She *Walks* in *Beauty*

GC GRAND CENTRAL PUBLISHING

NEW YORK   BOSTON

She *Walks* in *Beauty*

A Woman's Journey Through Poems

SELECTED AND INTRODUCED BY

Caroline Kennedy

Grand Central Publishing
Hachette Book Group
237 Park Avenue
New York, NY 10017

www.HachetteBookGroup.com

Printed in the United States of America

RRD-C

Originally published in hardcover by Hyperion.

First Grand Central Publishing Edition: July 2014
10 9 8 7 6 5 4 3 2 1

Grand Central Publishing is a division of Hachette Book Group, Inc.
The Grand Central Publishing name and logo is a trademark of Hachette Book Group, Inc.

The publisher is not responsible for websites (or their content) that are not owned by the publisher.

Book design by Shubhani Sarkar

Library of Congress Cataloging-in-Publication Data

She walks in beauty : a woman's Journey through poems / selected and introduced by Caroline Kennedy. — 1st ed.
     p.cm.
ISBN: 978-1-4013-4145-9
1. Poetry—Collections. I. Kennedy, Caroline
    PN6101.S475 2011
    808.81—dc22
            2011002177

Grand Central Publishing ISBN: 978-1-4555-8901-2

Contents

She walks in beauty   GEORGE GORDON, LORD BYRON   *1*

INTRODUCTION   *3*

FALLING IN LOVE

A Very Valentine   GERTRUDE STEIN   *9*

Song   JOHN KEATS   *10*

I Do Not Love Thee   HON. CAROLINE NORTON   *11*

From *Hero and Leander*   CHRISTOPHER MARLOWE   *12*

Love's Philosophy   PERCY BYSSHE SHELLEY   *13*

Having a Coke with You   FRANK O'HARA   *14*

Symptom Recital   DOROTHY PARKER   *16*

To Aphrodite of the Flowers, at Knossos   SAPPHO   *17*

Come to the Orchard in Spring   RUMI   *18*

Little Clown, My Heart   SANDRA CISNEROS   *19*

MAKING LOVE

Don't try to rush things—from *Poem 41*   ANTONIO MACHADO   *23*

From *From June to December*   WENDY COPE   *24*

Wild Nights—Wild Nights!   EMILY DICKINSON   *25*

may I feel said he   E. E. CUMMINGS   *26*

When He Pressed His Lips   STEVE KOWIT   *28*

Corinna's Going a-Maying	ROBERT HERRICK	*29*
The Weather-Cock Points South	AMY LOWELL	*32*
To His Mistress Going to Bed	JOHN DONNE	*33*
The Song of Solomon 2:1–17, 3:1–5		*35*
Final Soliloquy of the Interior Paramour	WALLACE STEVENS	*38*
Variation on the Word Sleep	MARGARET ATWOOD	*39*
After Making Love We Hear Footsteps	GALWAY KINNELL	*41*
It Is Marvellous . . .	ELIZABETH BISHOP	*42*
White Heliotrope	ARTHUR SYMONS	*43*
Youth	OSIP MANDELSTAM, TRANSLATED BY W. S. MERWIN	*44*

BREAKING UP

Lilacs	KATHERINE GARRISON CHAPIN	*47*
Unfortunate Coincidence	DOROTHY PARKER	*48*
The Philosopher	EDNA ST. VINCENT MILLAY	*49*
From *Summer with Monika*	ROGER McGOUGH	*50*
I'm Going to Georgia	FOLK SONG	*51*
A Type of Loss	INGEBORG BACHMANN	*52*
On Monsieur's Departure	QUEEN ELIZABETH I	*53*
The Eaten Heart—from The Knight of Curtesy		*54*
My life closed twice before its close—	EMILY DICKINSON	*58*
When We Two Parted	GEORGE GORDON, LORD BYRON	*59*
Well, I Have Lost You	EDNA ST. VINCENT MILLAY	*61*
What lips my lips have kissed, and where, and why (Sonnet XLIII)	EDNA ST. VINCENT MILLAY	*62*

"No, Thank You, John"	CHRISTINA ROSSETTI	63
when you have forgotten Sunday: the love story	GWENDOLYN BROOKS	65
The End	ELIZABETH ALEXANDER	67

MARRIAGE

The Passionate Shepherd to His Love	CHRISTOPHER MARLOWE	73
Marriage	GREGORY CORSO	74
From The Countess of Pembroke's Arcadia	SIR PHILIP SIDNEY	78
i carry your heart with me (i carry it in	E. E. CUMMINGS	79
To My Dear and Loving Husband	ANNE BRADSTREET	80
To Margo	GAVIN EWART	81
A Word to Husbands	OGDEN NASH	82
To the Ladies	LADY MARY CHUDLEIGH	83
The Female of the Species	RUDYARD KIPLING	84
From Paradise Lost	JOHN MILTON	87
The Good Wife	PROVERBS 31:10−31	91
My Last Duchess	ROBERT BROWNING	94
To Speak of Woe That Is in Marriage	ROBERT LOWELL	96
From a Survivor	ADRIENNE RICH	97
Letter from My Wife	NAZIM HIKMET	99
To Paula in Late Spring	W. S. MERWIN	101
A Farmer's Calendar	VIETNAMESE FOLK POEM	102

LOVE ITSELF

A Birthday	CHRISTINA ROSSETTI	*105*
June Light	RICHARD WILBUR	*106*
Protocols	VIKRAM SETH	*107*
Jamesian	THOM GUNN	*108*
From *Proverbs and Song Verse*	ANTONIO MACHADO	*109*
Sonnet XLIII: How Do I Love Thee?	ELIZABETH BARRETT BROWNING	*110*
XLIV: You must know that I do not love and that I love you	PABLO NERUDA	*111*
Code Poem for the French Resistance	LEO MARKS	*112*
The Smaller Orchid	AMY CLAMPITT	*113*
Sonnet 116	WILLIAM SHAKESPEARE	*114*
Out beyond ideas of wrongdoing	RUMI	*115*
The Emperor	MATTHEW ROHRER	*116*
Late Fragment	RAYMOND CARVER	*117*
From *The First Morning of the Second World*	DELMORE SCHWARTZ	*118*
1 Corinthians 13:1–13		*121*

WORK

weaponed woman	GWENDOLYN BROOKS	*125*
Night Waitress	LYNDA HULL	*126*
In an Iridescent Time	RUTH STONE	*129*
Madam and Her Madam	LANGSTON HUGHES	*130*
Letters from Storyville	NATASHA TRETHEWEY	*131*
Lineage	MARGARET WALKER	*134*

I Want You Women Up North to Know	TILLIE OLSEN	*135*
PS Education	ELLEN HAGAN	*139*
At the Café	PATRICIA KIRKPATRICK	*141*
Worked Late on a Tuesday Night	DEBORAH GARRISON	*142*
The Age of Great Vocations	ALANE ROLLINGS	*144*
Defining Worlds	G. Y. BAXTER	*147*
What's That Smell in the Kitchen?	MARGE PIERCY	*149*
Father Grumble	FOLK SONG	*150*
Epitaph	ANONYMOUS	*152*

BEAUTY, CLOTHES, AND THINGS OF THIS WORLD

Antony and Cleopatra, II, ii, 191–232	WILLIAM SHAKESPEARE	*157*
What Do Women Want?	KIM ADDONIZIO	*160*
The Catch	RICHARD WILBUR	*161*
Cosmetics Do No Good	STEVE KOWIT	*163*
Face Lift	SYLVIA PLATH	*164*
Fatigue	HILAIRE BELLOC	*166*
The Great Lover	RUPERT BROOKE	*167*
Patterns	AMY LOWELL	*170*
Crocheted Bag	ROSEMARY CATACALOS	*174*
Delight in Disorder	ROBERT HERRICK	*175*
The Rhodora	RALPH WALDO EMERSON	*176*
Roses Only	MARIANNE MOORE	*177*
Eagle Poem	JOY HARJO	*178*

MOTHERHOOD

A Cradle Song	W. B. YEATS	*181*
Notes from the Delivery Room	LINDA PASTAN	*182*
Socks	SHARON OLDS	*184*
High School Senior	SHARON OLDS	*185*
Nobody Knows But Mother	MARY MORRISON	*186*
From *"Clearances,"* In Memoriam M.K.H. (1911–1984)	SEAMUS HEANEY	*188*
Woman's Work	JULIA ALVAREZ	*189*
if there are any heavens my mother will (all by herself)have	E. E. CUMMINGS	*190*
Somebody's Mother	MARY DOW BRINE	*191*
The Book of Ruth 1:16–17		*193*
The Dream That I Told My Mother-in-Law	ELIZABETH ALEXANDER	*194*
Mother's Closet	MAXINE SCATES	*196*
Ode	ELIZABETH ALEXANDER	*198*
Vietnam	WISLAWA SZYMBORSKA	*199*
A Child	MARY LAMB	*200*
blessing the boats	LUCILLE CLIFTON	*201*

SILENCE AND SOLITUDE

I'm happiest when most away	EMILY BRONTË	*205*
Keeping Things Whole	MARK STRAND	*206*
We All Know It	MARIANNE MOORE	*207*
As Much As You Can	CONSTANTINE P. CAVAFY	*209*
The Heart of a Woman	GEORGIA DOUGLAS JOHNSON	*210*
Sense of Something Coming	RAINER MARIA RILKE	*211*

Death, Etc.	MAXINE KUMIN	*212*
From *When One Has Lived a Long Time Alone*	GALWAY KINNELL	*215*
Zazen on Ching-t'ing Mountain	LI PO	*217*
The Poems of Our Climate	WALLACE STEVENS	*218*

GROWING UP AND GROWING OLD

You Begin	MARGARET ATWOOD	*221*
Grown-up	EDNA ST. VINCENT MILLAY	*223*
Puberty—With Capital Letters	ELLEN HAGAN	*224*
Bra Shopping	PARNESHIA JONES	*225*
Hairwashing	JULIA ALVAREZ	*229*
The Summer Day	MARY OLIVER	*230*
Living	DENISE LEVERTOV	*231*
I stepped from plank to plank	EMILY DICKINSON	*232*
to my last period	LUCILLE CLIFTON	*233*
lumpectomy eve	LUCILLE CLIFTON	*234*
Older, Younger, Both	JOYCE SUTPHEN	*235*
Survivor	ROGER McGOUGH	*236*
You Can't Have It All	BARBARA RAS	*237*
Sign	MARGE PIERCY	*239*
The Greatest Love	ANNA SWIR	*240*
Time	MARY URSULA BETHELL	*241*
Going Blind	RAINER MARIA RILKE	*242*
Old Woman	ELIZABETH JENNINGS	*243*
Let It Be Forgotten	SARA TEASDALE	*244*
Courage	ANNE SEXTON	*245*

DEATH AND GRIEF

We know this much	SAPPHO	249
The Bustle in a House	EMILY DICKINSON	250
Never More Will the Wind	H. D.	251
Grief	ELIZABETH BARRETT BROWNING	252
The Widow's Lament in Springtime	WILLIAM CARLOS WILLIAMS	253
Companion	JO McDOUGALL	254
Remember	CHRISTINA ROSSETTI	255
From *To W. P.*	GEORGE SANTAYANA	256
To Death	OLIVER ST. JOHN GOGARTY	257
That it is a road	ARIWARA NO NARIHARA	258
From *In Memoriam A. H. H.*	ALFRED, LORD TENNYSON	259
Reconciliation	WALT WHITMAN	260

FRIENDSHIP

A Poem of Friendship	NIKKI GIOVANNI	263
Letter to N.Y.	ELIZABETH BISHOP	264
On Gifts for Grace	BERNADETTE MAYER	266
Love	ROY CROFT	267
To Hayley	WILLIAM BLAKE	269
A Poison Tree	WILLIAM BLAKE	270
August	LOUISE GLÜCK	271
Summer at the Beach	LOUISE GLÜCK	273
Girlfriends	ELLEN DORÉ WATSON	275

Woman Friend	JULIA ALVAREZ	276
My Friend's Divorce	NAOMI SHIHAB NYE	278
Chocolate	RITA DOVE	279
Magnificat	MICHÈLE ROBERTS	280
Secret Lives	BARBARA RAS	282
To Flush, My Dog	ELIZABETH BARRETT BROWNING	284

HOW TO LIVE

May 2	DAVID LEHMAN	293
From a Letter to His Daughter	RALPH WALDO EMERSON	294
To be of use	MARGE PIERCY	295
Leap Before You Look	W. H. AUDEN	296
Try to Praise the Mutilated World	ADAM ZAGAJEWSKI	297
Leisure	W. H. DAVIES	298
The Waking	THEODORE ROETHKE	299
September, 1918	AMY LOWELL	300
6 A.M. Thoughts	DICK DAVIS	301
A Minor Bird	ROBERT FROST	302
May today there be peace within	ST. TERESA OF AVILA	303
The Bacchae Chorus	EURIPIDES	305
The Dawn	W. B. YEATS	307
Don't Quit	UNKNOWN	308
All Things Pass	LAO-TZU	309
Simple Gifts	ANONYMOUS (SHAKER HYMN)	310

24th September 1945   NAZIM HIKMET   *311*

The Journey   MARY OLIVER   *312*

Ithaka   CONSTANTINE P. CAVAFY   *314*

The Colder the Air   ELIZABETH BISHOP   *316*

ACKNOWLEDGMENTS   *319*

CREDITS   *321*

She *Walks* in *Beauty*

She walks in beauty

GEORGE GORDON, LORD BYRON

She walks in beauty, like the night
   Of cloudless climes and starry skies;
And all that's best of dark and bright
   Meet in her aspect and her eyes:
Thus mellow'd to that tender light
   Which heaven to gaudy day denies.

One shade the more, one ray the less,
   Had half impair'd the nameless grace
Which waves in every raven tress,
   Or softly lightens o'er her face;
Where thoughts serenely sweet express
   How pure, how dear their dwelling-place.

And on that cheek, and o'er that brow,
   So soft, so calm, yet eloquent,
The smiles that win, the tints that glow,
   But tell of days in goodness spent,
A mind at peace with all below,
   A heart whose love is innocent!

INTRODUCTION

*T*HIS BOOK BEGAN around the time I turned fifty. Like my friends who had been there before me, I dreaded it for months, and was relieved when it was over and life seemed much the same as before. One of the nicest things that happened was that three friends sent me poems to mark the occasion. One poem was about love, one helped me cope with loss, and the third spoke to ways of being. I kept them and passed them on to others when the time seemed right. To me, that's the gift of poetry—it shapes an endless conversation about the most important things in life.

Creating an anthology of poems centered around the stages of a woman's life still seems like an unlikely project to me. I have shied away from the personal genre of literature, and never thought that growing old would be something I would do. Perhaps that's because, in my family, my cousins and I still refer to our parents' generation as "the grown-ups," although most of us are in our fifties. But there seemed to be something profoundly different about hitting the middle-age mark—a sense of accomplishment, an emotional reckoning, and a feeling of renewed possibility about the future. All that, and a tiny terror of sliding down the hill into a crumpled heap of old age. Working on this book reminded me that the personal is universal, being a woman is a profound part of who I am, and sharing experiences and emotions is the best way we can help ourselves and others.

Approaching middle age made me appreciate my deep connection to the women I have grown up with, worked with, and whose children have grown up with mine. We have learned what is important, we can look back as well as forward, and we have the chance to weave the choices we have already made into the changes we want to bring to our lives. Reading poems can help bring clarity and insight to emotions that can be confusing or contradictory.

Women have always been at the center of poetry—throughout history we have been its inspiration, and more recently, women are the authors of the most profound poetry of our time. One of the oldest known poets in the world is a woman—Sappho—and her fragments of verse are as emotionally piercing today as the work of many modern writers. The love poetry of medieval troubadours, Renaissance playwrights, and Romantic poets (almost exclusively men) celebrated female beauty and mystery; conquest, heartbreak, and desire. In the twentieth century, women poets gave voice to the pain and joy, relationships and loneliness, the work and the life of women. In today's world, as women struggle to balance work and family, to be good mothers and friends, to care for our children and our parents, poetry can help us accept our limitations, and inspire us to overcome them. In a world where language is too often used to manipulate, poems can help us find our authentic voice.

The book is divided into sections that seem broad enough to encompass the milestones in a woman's life—"Falling in Love," "Breaking Up," "Marriage," "Motherhood," "Death and Grief"— but they are intended as helpful, if arbitrary, dividers. Other sections are about some of the things that make us happy, like "Friendship" or "Beauty." My favorite section is the one titled "How to Live." It includes the poems that started this book, and many others, each containing wisdom that has helped me on my own journey.

Collecting these poems reminded me that when I was younger, I thought my task was to forge ahead and succeed as an individual. But growing older has helped me realize that our success lies in our relationships—with the family we are born into, the friends we make, the people we fall in love with, and the children we have. Sometimes we struggle, sometimes we adapt, and at other times we set a course for others to follow. We are all leaders and followers in our lives. We are constantly learning from and teaching one another. We learn, too, that the most important work is not done by those who seem the most important, but by those who care the most.

Women have always been the weavers of the world, literally and figuratively. We weave people together, we weave the experiences of life into patterns, and we weave our stories into words. Poetry has been one of the ways we do this. Poems distill our deepest emotions into a very few words—words that we can remember, carry with us, and share with others as we talk and weave the cloth of life.

FALLING IN LOVE

T HERE ARE SO MANY WAYS TO FALL IN LOVE—and so many people to fall in love with. When I was young, I went to a convent school, read historical romances, and dreamed of the day a modern Scarlet Pimpernel would sweep me off my feet, but really, I was only in love with my pony. As a result, in high school, I was way behind the girls who had already figured out the basics of human-to-human love and despaired of ever having a boyfriend. One of the reassuring things my mother said to me was that if you love someone, that person will love you back. Although there is not much evidence to support that theory, I decided to believe it, and eventually, like all mothers, she turned out to be right.

Now, as I watch my children fall in love, it brings back the memories of excitement, uncertainty, adventure, and the joy of belonging to someone. Falling in love means you aren't a child anymore and, as Rumi writes in "Come to the Orchard in Spring," nothing else matters. In these poems, John Keats captures the essence of desire, Percy Bysshe Shelley expresses the delights of kissing, and Christopher Marlowe rules out anything but love at first sight.

Throughout the ages, one of poetry's challenges has been to express mystical experiences in language. Falling in love is a

series of moments in which the ordinary becomes extraordinary. Those moments are not continuous, but the sense of union with another person is just about the best thing there is. Perhaps that is why Dorothy Parker and Sandra Cisneros celebrate our need to do it over and over again.

A Very Valentine

GERTRUDE STEIN

Very fine is my valentine.
Very fine and very mine.
Very mine is my valentine very mine and very fine.
Very fine is my valentine and mine, very fine very mine and
  mine is my valentine.

Song

JOHN KEATS

O blush not so! O blush not so!
   Or I shall think you knowing;
And if you smile the blushing while,
   Then maidenheads are going.

There's a blush for won't, and a blush for shan't,
   And a blush for having done it:
There's a blush for thought, and a blush for naught,
   And a blush for just begun it.

O sigh not so! O sigh not so!
   For it sounds of Eve's sweet pippin;
By those loosened lips you have tasted the pips
   And fought in an amorous nipping.

Will you play once more at nice-cut-core,
   For it only will last our youth out?
And we have the prime of the kissing time,
   We have not one sweet tooth out.

There's a sigh for yes, and a sigh for no,
   And a sigh for I can't bear it!
O what can be done, shall we stay or run?
   O, cut the sweet apple and share it!

I Do Not Love Thee

THE HONORABLE CAROLINE ELIZABETH SARAH NORTON

I do not love thee!—no! I do not love thee!
    And yet when thou art absent I am sad;
And envy even the bright blue sky above thee,
    Whose quiet stars may see thee and be glad.

I do not love thee!—yet, I know not why,
    Whate'er thou dost seems still well done, to me:
And often in my solitude I sigh
    That those I do love are not more like thee!

I do not love thee!—yet, when thou art gone,
    I hate the sound (though those who speak be dear)
Which breaks the lingering echo of the tone
    Thy voice of music leaves upon my ear.

I do not love thee!—yet thy speaking eyes,
    With their deep, bright and most expressive blue,
Between me and the midnight heaven arise,
    Oftener than any eyes I ever knew.

I know I do not love thee! yet, alas!
    Others will scarcely trust my candid heart;
And oft I catch them smiling as they pass,
    Because they see me gazing where thou art.

From *Hero and Leander*

CHRISTOPHER MARLOWE

It lies not in our power to love or hate,
For will in us is over-ruled by fate.
When two are stripped, long ere the course begin
We wish that one should lose, the other win;
And one especially do we affect
Of two gold ingots, like in each respect.
The reason no man knows; let it suffice,
What we behold is censured by our eyes.
Where both deliberate, the love is slight;
Who ever loved, that loved not at first sight?

Love's Philosophy

PERCY BYSSHE SHELLEY

The fountains mingle with the river
   And the rivers with the Ocean,
The winds of Heaven mix for ever
   With a sweet emotion;
Nothing in the world is single;
   All things by a law divine
In one spirit meet and mingle.
   Why not I with thine?—

See the mountains kiss high Heaven
   And the waves clasp one another;
No sister-flower would be forgiven
   If it disdained its brother;
And the sunlight clasps the earth
   And the moonbeams kiss the sea:
What is all this sweet work worth
   If thou kiss not me?

Having a Coke with You

FRANK O'HARA

is even more fun than going to San Sebastian, Irún, Hendaye,
   Biarritz, Bayonne
or being sick to my stomach on the Travesera de Gracia in
   Barcelona
partly because in your orange shirt you look like a better happier
   St. Sebastian
partly because of my love for you, partly because of your love for
   yoghurt
partly because of the fluorescent orange tulips around the birches
partly because of the secrecy our smiles take on before people
   and statuary
it is hard to believe when I'm with you that there can be
   anything as still
as solemn as unpleasantly definitive as statuary when right in
   front of it
in the warm New York 4 o'clock light we are drifting back and
   forth
between each other like a tree breathing through its spectacles

and the portrait show seems to have no faces in it at all, just
   paint
you suddenly wonder why in the world anyone ever did them
                                                      I look
at you and I would rather look at you than all the portraits in
   the world
except possibly for the *Polish Rider* occasionally and anyway it's in
   the Frick
which thank heavens you haven't gone to yet so we can go
   together the first time

and the fact that you move so beautifully more or less takes care
  of Futurism
just as at home I never think of the *Nude Descending a Staircase*
  or
at a rehearsal a single drawing of Leonardo or Michelangelo that
  used to wow me
and what good does all the research of the Impressionists do
  them
when they never got the right person to stand near the tree when
  the sun sank
or for that matter Marino Marini when he didn't pick the rider
  as carefully
as the horse
                it seems they were all cheated of some marvellous
  experience
which is not going to go wasted on me which is why I'm telling
  you about it

Symptom Recital

DOROTHY PARKER

I do not like my state of mind;
I'm bitter, querulous, unkind.
I hate my legs, I hate my hands,
I do not yearn for lovelier lands.
I dread the dawn's recurrent light;
I hate to go to bed at night.
I snoot at simple, earnest folk.
I cannot take the gentlest joke.
I find no peace in paint or type.
My world is but a lot of tripe.
I'm disillusioned, empty-breasted.
For what I think, I'd be arrested.
I am not sick, I am not well.
My quondam dreams are shot to hell.
My soul is crushed, my spirit sore;
I do not like me any more.
I cavil, quarrel, grumble, grouse.
I ponder on the narrow house.
I shudder at the thought of men . . .
I'm due to fall in love again.

To Aphrodite of the Flowers, at Knossos

SAPPHO

Leave Crete and come to this holy temple
where the pleasant grove of apple trees
circles an altar smoking with frank-
     incense.

Here roses leave shadow on the ground
and cold springs babble through apple branches
where shuddering leaves pour down pro-
     found sleep.

In our meadow where horses graze
and wild flowers of spring blossom,
anise shoots fill the air with a-
     roma.

And here, Queen Aphrodite, pour
heavenly nectar into gold cups
and fill them gracefully with sud-
     den joy.

Come to the Orchard in Spring

RUMI

Come to the orchard in Spring.
There is light and wine, and sweethearts
   in the pomegranate flowers.

If you do not come, these do not matter.
If you do come, these do not matter.

Little Clown, My Heart

SANDRA CISNEROS

Little clown, my heart,
Spangled again and lopsided,
Handstands and Peking pirouettes,
Backflips snapping open like
A carpenter's hinged ruler,

Little gimp-footed hurray,
Paper parasol of pleasures,
Fleshy undertongue of sorrows,
Sweet potato plant of my addictions,

Acapulco cliff-diver *corazón,*
Fine as an obsidian dagger,
Alley-oop and here we go
Into the froth, my life,
Into the flames!

MAKING LOVE

MY CHILDREN WERE HORRIFIED to see the words "Making Love" in the Contents for this book. After all, there are few things more disturbing than the idea of your parents being engaged in any sort of romantic activity. However, as I tried to point out, in literature the phrase "making love" refers to courtship, flirtation, and other aspects of romantic pursuit and intimacy. But my words fell on disbelieving ears with fingers sticking out of them—they would hear none of it.

Longing for love, the anticipation of a big night, the accoutrements of romance—handkerchiefs, valentines, corsages, lockets—keepsakes and mementos all have the power to conjure up intense emotion. Today, when popular culture often demeans women and promotes graphic and vulgar descriptions of sex, love poetry can seem old-fashioned and irrelevant. But if we open our minds and listen, we will find unbelievably suggestive images and metaphors in poems that are thousands of years old. Though much is left to the imagination, and perhaps because it is, there are few more evocative lines in all of literature than the Song of Solomon. I doubt I am the only person who has squirmed when it is read aloud at a wedding. Likewise, John Donne, writing in the late 1500s, was a minister and a holy man, but the fervor of his love poetry is unmatched, and those who prefer explicit descriptions of "making love" won't be disappointed.

Poems about amorous activities are often lighthearted and funny. In "may I feel said he," e. e. cummings captures the guilty pleasures of an illicit affair. Galway Kinnell writes ruefully of the ability of young children to interrupt their parents at inappropriate moments, and Antonio Machado wryly advises lovers to proceed slowly.

Poets like Wallace Stevens in "Final Soliloquy of the Interior Paramour" and W. S. Merwin in his translation of "Youth" create in a very few words a world of two lovers. They distill passion and evoke moments of peaceful joy and a universe of all-encompassing love. It is up to the reader to take the concept of "making love" forward from there.

Don't try to rush things
from *Poem 41*

ANTONIO MACHADO

Don't try to rush things:
for the cup to run over,
it must first be filled.

From *From June to December*
Summer Villanelle
WENDY COPE

You know exactly what to do—
Your kiss, your fingers on my thigh—
I think of little else but you.

It's bliss to have a lover who,
Touching one shoulder, makes me sigh—
You know exactly what to do.

You make me happy through and through,
The way the sun lights up the sky—
I think of little else but you.

I hardly sleep—an hour or two;
I can't eat much and this is why—
You know exactly what to do.

The movie in my mind is blue—
As June runs into warm July
I think of little else but you.

But is it love? And is it true?
Who cares? This much I can't deny:
You know exactly what to do;
I think of little else but you.

. . .

Wild Nights—Wild Nights!

EMILY DICKINSON

Wild Nights—Wild Nights!
Were I with thee
Wild Nights should be
Our luxury!

Futile—the Winds—
To a Heart in port—
Done with the Compass—
Done with the Chart!

Rowing in Eden—
Ah, the Sea!
Might I but moor—Tonight—
In Thee!

may i feel said he

E. E. CUMMINGS

may i feel said he
(i'll squeal said she
just once said he)
it's fun said she

(may i touch said he
how much said she
a lot said he)
why not said she

(let's go said he
not too far said she
what's too far said he
where you are said she)

may i stay said he
(which way said she
like this said he
if you kiss said she

may i move said he
is it love said she)
if you're willing said he
(but you're killing said she

but it's life said he
but your wife said she
now said he)
ow said she

(tiptop said he
don't stop said she
oh no said he)
go slow said she

(cccome?said he
ummm said she)
you're divine!said he
(you are Mine said she)

When He Pressed His Lips

after Vikatanitamba

STEVE KOWIT

When he pressed his lips to my mouth
the knot fell open of itself.
When he pressed them to my throat
the dress slipped to my feet.
So much I know—but
when his lips touched my breast
everything, I swear,
down to his very name,
became so much confused
that I am still,
dear friends,
unable to recount
(as much as I would care to)
what delights
were next bestowed upon me
& by whom.

Corinna's Going a-Maying

ROBERT HERRICK

Get up, get up for shame! the blooming morn
Upon her wings presents the god unshorn.
   See how Aurora throws her fair
   Fresh-quilted colours through the air:
   Get up, sweet slug-a-bed, and see
   The dew-bespangling herb and tree.
Each flower has wept, and bowed toward the east,
Above an hour since; yet you not drest,
   Nay! not so much as out of bed?
   When all the birds have matins said,
   And sung their thankful hymns, 'tis sin,
   Nay, profanation to keep in,
Whenas a thousand virgins on this day
Spring sooner than the lark to fetch in May.

Rise and put on your foliage, and be seen
To come forth, like the spring-time, fresh and green,
   And sweet as Flora. Take no care
   For jewels for your gown or hair:
   Fear not; the leaves will strew
   Gems in abundance upon you:
Besides, the childhood of the day has kept,
Against you come, some orient pearls unwept.
   Come, and receive them while the light
   Hangs on the dew-locks of the night:
   And Titan on the eastern hill
   Retires himself, or else stands still
Till you come forth. Wash, dress, be brief in praying:
Few beads are best when once we go a-Maying.

Come, my Corinna, come; and coming, mark
How each field turns a street, each street a park
   Made green and trimmed with trees: see how
   Devotion gives each house a bough
   Or branch; each porch, each door, ere this,
   An ark, a tabernacle is,
Made up of white-thorn neatly interwove,
As if here were those cooler shades of love.
   Can such delights be in the street
   And open fields, and we not see't?
   Come, we'll abroad: and let's obey
   The proclamation made for May,
And sin no more, as we have done, by staying;
But, my Corinna, come, let's go a-Maying.

There's not a budding boy or girl this day
But is got up and gone to bring in May.
   A deal of youth ere this is come
   Back, and with white-thorn laden home.
   Some have dispatched their cakes and cream,
   Before that we have left to dream:
And some have wept and wooed, and plighted troth,
And chose their priest, ere we can cast off sloth:
   Many a green-gown has been given;
   Many a kiss, both odd and even;
   Many a glance too has been sent
   From out the eye, love's firmament:
Many a jest told of the keys betraying
This night, and locks picked: yet we're not a-Maying!

Come, let us go, while we are in our prime,
And take the harmless folly of the time!
   We shall grow old apace, and die

Before we know our liberty.
Our life is short, and our days run
As fast away as does the sun.
And as a vapour or a drop of rain,
Once lost, can ne'er be found again:
So when or you or I are made
A fable, song, or fleeting shade,
All love, all liking, all delight
Lies drowned with us in endless night.
Then, while time serves, and we are but decaying,
Come, my Corinna, come, let's go a-Maying.

The Weather-Cock Points South

AMY LOWELL

I put your leaves aside,
One by one:
The stiff, broad outer leaves;
The smaller ones,
Pleasant to touch, veined with purple;
The glazed inner leaves.

One by one
Parted you from your leaves,
Until you stood up like a white flower
Swaying slightly in the evening wind.

White flower,
Flower of wax, of jade, of unstreaked agate;
Flower with surfaces of ice,
With shadows faintly crimson.
Where in all the garden is there such a flower?
The stars crowd through the lilac leaves
To look at you.
The low moon brightens you with silver.

The bud is more than the calyx.
There is nothing to equal a white bud,
Of no color, and of all,
Burnished by moonlight,
Thrust upon by a softly-swinging wind.

To His Mistress Going to Bed

JOHN DONNE

Come, Madam, come, all rest my powers defy,
Until I labour, I in labour lie.
The foe oft-times having the foe in sight,
Is tir'd with standing though he never fight.
Off with that girdle, like heaven's zone glistering,
But a far fairer world incompassing.
Unpin that spangled breastplate which you wear,
That th'eyes of busy fools may be stopped there.
Unlace your self, for that harmonious chime,
Tells me from you, that now it is bed time.
Off with that happy busk, which I envy,
That still can be, and still can stand so nigh.
Your gown going off, such beauteous state reveals,
As when from flowry meads th'hill's shadow steals.
Off with that wiry Coronet and show
The hairy diadem which on you doth grow:
Now off with those shoes, and then safely tread
In this love's hallow'd temple, this soft bed.
In such white robes, heaven's angels us'd to be
Receiv'd by men; thou angel bringst with thee
A heaven like Mahomet's paradise; and though
Ill spirits walk in white, we eas'ly know,
By this these angels from an evil sprite,
Those set our hairs, but these our flesh upright.
   Licence my roving hands, and let them go,
Before, behind, between, above, below.
O my America! my new-found-land,
My kingdom, safeliest when with one man mann'd,
My mine of precious stones, my empery,

How blest am I in this discovering thee!
To enter in these bonds, is to be free;
Then where my hand is set, my seal shall be.

    Full nakedness! All joys are due to thee,
As souls unbodied, bodies uncloth'd must be,
To taste whole joys. Gems which you women use
Are like Atlanta's balls, cast in men's views,
That when a fool's eye lighteth on a gem,
His earthly soul may covet theirs, not them.
Like pictures, or like books' gay coverings made
For lay-men, are all women thus array'd;
Themselves are mystic books, which only we
(Whom their imputed grace will dignify)
Must see reveal'd. Then since that I may know;
As liberally, as to a midwife, show
Thyself: cast all, yea, this white linen hence,
Here is no penance, much less innocence.

    To teach thee, I am naked first; why then
What needst thou have more covering than a man?

I am the rose of Sharon,
And the lily of the valleys.
As the lily among thorns,
So is my love among the daughters.
As the apple tree among the trees of the wood,
So is my beloved among the sons.

I sat down under his shadow with great delight,
And his fruit was sweet to my taste.
He brought me to the banqueting house,
And his banner over me was love.

Stay me with flagons, comfort me with apples
For I am sick of love.
His left hand is under my head,
And his right hand doth embrace me.

I charge you, O ye daughters of Jerusalem,
By the roes, and by the hinds of the field,
That ye stir not up, nor awake my love,
Till he please.

The voice of my beloved!
Behold, he cometh leaping upon the mountains,
Skipping upon the hills.
My beloved is like a roe or a young hart.
Behold, he standeth behind our wall,
He looketh forth at the windows,
Showing himself through the lattice.
My beloved spake, and said unto me,

"Rise up, my love, my fair one, and come away.
For, lo, the winter is past,
The rain is over and gone;
The flowers appear on the earth;
The time of the singing of birds is come,
And the voice of the turtle is heard in our land;
The fig tree putteth forth her green figs,
And the vines with the tender grape give a good smell.
Arise, my love, my fair one, and come away.

"O my dove, that art in the clefts of the rock,
In the secret places of the stairs,
Let me see thy countenance,
Let me hear thy voice;
For sweet is thy voice,
And thy countenance is comely."

Take us the foxes,
The little foxes, that spoil the vines:
For our vines have tender grapes.

My beloved is mine, and I am his:
He feedeth among the lilies.
Until the day break, and the shadows flee away,
Turn, my beloved, and be thou like a roe
Or a young hart upon the mountains of Bether.

By night on my bed I sought him whom my soul loveth:
I sought him, but I found him not.

I will rise now,
And go about the city in the streets,
And in the broad ways I will seek him whom my soul loveth:

I sought him, but I found him not.
The watchmen that go about the city found me:
To whom I said, "Saw ye him whom my soul loveth?"

It was but a little that I passed from them,
But I found him whom my soul loveth:
I held him, and would not let him go,
Until I had brought him into my mother's house,
And into the chamber of her that conceived me.

I charge you, O ye daughters of Jerusalem,
By the roes, and by the hinds of the field,
That ye stir not up, nor awake my love,
Till he please.

Final Soliloquy of the Interior Paramour

WALLACE STEVENS

Light the first light of evening, as in a room
In which we rest and, for small reason, think
The world imagined is the ultimate good.

This is, therefore, the intensest rendezvous.
It is in that thought that we collect ourselves,
Out of all the indifferences, into one thing:

Within a single thing, a single shawl
Wrapped tightly round us, since we are poor, a warmth,
A light, a power, the miraculous influence.

Here, now, we forget each other and ourselves.
We feel the obscurity of an order, a whole,
A knowledge, that which arranged the rendezvous.

Within its vital boundary, in the mind.
We say God and the imagination are one . . .
How high that highest candle lights the dark.

Out of this same light, out of the central mind,
We make a dwelling in the evening air,
In which being there together is enough.

Variation on the Word Sleep

MARGARET ATWOOD

I would like to watch you sleeping,
which may not happen.
I would like to watch you,
sleeping. I would like to sleep
with you, to enter
your sleep as its smooth dark wave
slides over my head

and walk with you through that lucent
wavering forest of bluegreen leaves
with its watery sun & three moons
towards the cave where you must descend,
towards your worst fear

I would like to give you the silver
branch, the small white flower, the one
word that will protect you
from the grief at the center
of your dream, from the grief
at the center. I would like to follow
you up the long stairway
again & become
the boat that would row you back
carefully, a flame
in two cupped hands
to where your body lies
beside me, and you enter
it as easily as breathing in

I would like to be the air
that inhabits you for a moment
only. I would like to be that unnoticed
& that necessary.

After Making Love We Hear Footsteps

GALWAY KINNELL

For I can snore like a bullhorn
or play loud music
or sit up talking with any reasonably sober Irishman
and Fergus will only sink deeper
into his dreamless sleep, which goes by all in one flash,
but let there be that heavy breathing
or a stifled come-cry anywhere in the house
and he will wrench himself awake
and make for it on the run—as now, we lie together,
after making love, quiet, touching along the length of our bodies,
familiar touch of the long-married,
and he appears—in his baseball pajamas, it happens,
the neck opening so small he has to screw them on—
and flops down between us and hugs us and snuggles himself
    to sleep,
his face gleaming with satisfaction at being this very child.

In the half darkness we look at each other
and smile
and touch arms across this little, startlingly muscled body—
this one whom habit of memory propels to the ground of his making,
sleeper only the mortal sounds can sing awake,
this blessing love gives again into our arms.

It Is Marvellous . . .

ELIZABETH BISHOP

It is marvellous to wake up together
At the same minute; marvellous to hear
The rain begin suddenly all over the roof,
To feel the air clear
As if electricity had passed through it
From a black mesh of wires in the sky.
All over the roof the rain hisses,
And below, the light falling of kisses.

An electrical storm is coming or moving away;
It is the prickling air that wakes us up.
If lightning struck the house now, it would run
From the four blue china balls on top
Down the roof and down the rods all around us,
And we imagine dreamily
How the whole house caught in a bird-cage of lightning
Would be quite delightful rather than frightening;

And from the same simplified point of view
Of night and lying flat on one's back
All things might change equally easily,
Since always to warn us there must be these black
Electrical wires dangling. Without surprise
The world might change to something quite different,
As the air changes or the lightning comes without our blinking,
Change as our kisses are changing without our thinking.

White Heliotrope

ARTHUR SYMONS

The feverish room and that white bed,
The tumbled skirts upon a chair,
The novel flung half-open, where
Hat, hair-pins, puffs, and paints, are spread;

The mirror that has sucked your face
Into its secret deep of deeps,
And there mysteriously keeps
Forgotten memories of grace;

And you, half dressed and half awake,
Your slant eyes strangely watching me,
And I, who watch you drowsily,
With eyes that, having slept not, ache;

This (need one dread? nay, dare one hope?)
Will rise, a ghost of memory, if
Ever again my handkerchief
Is scented with White Heliotrope.

Youth

OSIP MANDELSTAM
Translated by W. S. Merwin

Through all of youth I was looking for you
without knowing what I was looking for

or what to call you I think I did not
even know I was looking how would I

have known you when I saw you as I did
time after time when you appeared to me

as you did naked offering yourself
entirely at that moment and you let

me breathe you touch you taste you knowing
no more than I did and only when I

began to think of losing you did I
recognize you when you were already

part memory part distance remaining
mine in the ways that I learn to miss you

from what we cannot hold the stars are made

BREAKING UP

*G*IRLFRIENDS ARE THE WORST," said my son morosely, after learning that his high school sweetheart didn't want to get back together with him after the summer. "She won't talk to me, not even on the phone," he said, shaking his head.

When I was his age, girls usually seemed to be the broken-hearted ones, chasing after some unavailable boy with hair down to his shoulders. Caught off guard by the idea that a teenage boy, rather than girl, would want to discuss a relationship and work through the issues, I quickly improvised some unconvincing maternal words of comfort. But we all go through the misery of breaking up. Even if we know a relationship isn't meant to last, it is still painful when it ends. Emily Dickinson puts it best when she writes, "Parting is all we know of heaven,/And all we need of hell."

These poems explore different kinds of endings. In "Unfortunate Coincidence," Dorothy Parker describes a relationship in which both parties know they are only pretending to be in love, whereas Edna St. Vincent Millay's poem "The Philosopher" was sent to me by a friend whose husband had been unfaithful.

My favorite metaphor for a past love affair is found in Edna St. Vincent Millay's two poems "Well, I Have Lost You" and Sonnet XLIII. In both, she compares being in love to summertime. In

Sonnet XLIII she writes, "I only know that summer sang in me/A little while, that in me sings no more." Like summer, love is full and abundant, and when it ends there is a sense of loss, but also the implicit knowledge that we will fall in love again when the time comes around.

After reading many poems about breaking up, it seems that male and female poets tend to focus on different aspects of the end of a relationship. I doubt women will be surprised that men write more often about the loss of face and the loss of power, while women tend to write about the loss of self. In her poem "On Monsieur's Departure," even Queen Elizabeth I, who understood and exercised almost absolute power, is reduced to a pitiful female creature after she breaks up with a male lover.

The most extreme expression of the desire for revenge is seen in the legend of "The Eaten Heart." The version here dates from a Middle English poem of the 1500s, but the legend appears in many cultures. The poem tells the story of a jealous husband who tricks his wife into eating her slain lover's heart and then tells her what she has done. After that, she kills herself. Even metaphorically, human relationships don't get much more twisted than that.

Hopefully, the world has become a little more civilized since then, and we can move through the stages of loss and grief that mark the end of a relationship in a more gradual and accepting way. Gwendolyn Brooks's poem, "when you have forgotten Sunday: the love story," and Elizabeth Alexander's "The End" both describe relationships in which eventually even the memory fades away. Then, we can understand what we have learned and begin the search for love again.

Lilacs

KATHERINE GARRISON CHAPIN

When I met my lover
  Lilacs were new,
He said, "I brought some lilacs,
  Lilacs for you."

I took them eagerly
  Laughing in surprise;
He said: "They are pretty
  Just like your eyes."

I pressed the pointed blossoms
  Close to my cheek,
And the smooth green leaves . . .
  But I couldn't speak.

How was I to tell him,
  Spring being new,
How say: "It is the lilacs
  I love, not you."

Unfortunate Coincidence

DOROTHY PARKER

By the time you swear you're his,
 Shivering and sighing,
And he vows his passion is
 Infinite, undying—
Lady, make a note of this:
 One of you is lying.

The Philosopher

EDNA ST. VINCENT MILLAY

And what are you that, wanting you,
I should be kept awake
As many nights as there are days
With weeping for your sake?

And what are you that, missing you,
As many days as crawl
I should be listening to the wind
And looking at the wall?

I know a man that's a braver man
And twenty men as kind,
And what are you, that you should be
The one man on my mind?

Yet women's ways are witless ways,
As any sage will tell—
And what am I, that I should love
So wisely and so well?

From *Summer with Monika*

ROGER McGOUGH

away from you
i feel a great emptiness
a gnawing loneliness

with you
i get that reassuring feeling
of wanting to escape

I'm Going to Georgia

I once loved a young man as dear as my life,
And ofttimes I told him I'd make him his wife.
I've fulfilled my promise, I made him his wife
And see what I've come to by being his wife.

   I'm going to Georgia,
   I'm going to roam,
   And if ever I get there,
   I'll make it my home.

My cheeks were once red, as red as a rose,
But now they are as pale as the lilies that grow;
My children all hungry and crying for bread;
My husband, a drunkard, Lord, I wish I were dead!

Come, all young ladies, take warning by me:
Never plant your affections on a green, young tree;
For the leaves will wither and the buds they will die;
Some young man might fool you as one has fooled I.

They'll hug you, they'll kiss you, they'll tell you more lies
Than the cross-ties on the railroad or the stars in the skies;
They'll tell you they love you like stars in the West
But along comes corn whiskey; they love it the best.

Go, build me a cabin on the mountain so high
Where the wild birds and turtledove can hear my sad cry.

A Type of Loss

INGEBORG BACHMANN

Jointly used: seasons, books and music.
The keys, the tea cups, the breadbasket, sheets
     and a bed.
A dowry of words, of gestures, brought along,
     used, spent.
Social manners observed. Said. Done. And always
     the hand extended.

With winter, a Vienna septet and with summer I've
     been in love.
With maps, a mountain hut, with a beach and
     a bed.
A cult filled with dates, promises made
     as if irrevocable,
enthused about Something and pious before Nothing,

(—the folded newspapers, cold ashes, the slip of paper
     with a jotted note)
fearless in religion, as the church was this bed.

From the seascape came my inexhaustible painting.
From the balcony, the people, my neighbors,
     were there to be greeted.
By the fireplace, in safety, my hair had its most exceptional
     color.
The doorbell ringing was the alarm for my joy.

It was not you I lost,
but the world.

On Monsieur's Departure

QUEEN ELIZABETH I

I grieve and dare not show my discontent,
I love and yet am forced to seem to hate,
I do, yet dare not say I ever meant,
I seem stark mute but inwardly do prate.
    I am and not, I freeze and yet am burned,
    Since from myself another self I turned.

My care is like my shadow in the sun,
Follows me flying, flies when I pursue it,
Stands and lies by me, doth what I have done.
His too familiar care doth make me rue it.
    No means I find to rid him from my breast,
    Till by the end of things it be supprest.

Some gentler passion slide into my mind,
For I am soft and made of melting snow;
Or be more cruel, love, and so be kind.
Let me or float or sink, be high or low.
    Or let me live with some more sweet content,
    Or die and so forget what love ere meant.

The Eaten Heart
from *The Knight of Curtesy*

"Make it sweet and delicate to eat
For it is for my lady bright.
If she guessed what was in this meat
Her heart would not be light."

The lord's words were truly spoke
The meat of woe and death
The lady did not know it though
And followed him across the hearth.

And when the lord sat down to eat
His lady at his side
The heart was served upon the plate
But it had grief inside.

"Madame, eat of this," he said,
"For it is dainty and pleasant."
The lady ate and was not dismayed
For of spice there was not want.

When the lady had eaten well
To her the lord said there,
"His heart you have eaten every morsel
Of your knight to whom you gave a lock of hair.

"As you can see, your knight is dead;
Madame, I tell you certainly.
That is his heart on which you fed.
Madame, at last we all must die."

When the lady heard the words he said
She cried, "My heart shall rend
Alas, I ever saw this day
Now, please God may my life end."

Up she rose with heart of woe
And straight to her chamber went;
She confessed devoutly so
That shortly she received the sacrament.

Mourning in her bed she lay
So pitiful was her moan.
"Alas, my own dear love," she said,
"Since you are dead, my life is gone.

"Have I taken your heart in my body
That meat to me is dear;
For sorrow alas I now must die
A noble knight without fear

"With me thy heart shall surely die
I have received the sacrament;
All earthly food I shall deny
In woe and pain, my life is spent."

Her complaint was piteous to hear.
"Goodbye my lord forever;
I die as true a wife to you
As any could be ever

"I am chaste of the knight of curtesy
And wrongfully are we brought to confusion

I am chaste of him and he of me
And of all other save you alone.

"My lord, you were to blame
For making me eat his heart;
But since it is buried in my body
I shall never eat any other meat.

"I have now received eternal food
Earthly meat will I never touch
Now realize what you have done
Have mercy on me—and believe."

With that the lady in front of all in sight
Yielded up her spirit with a moan;
The high god of heaven almighty
On us have mercy—every one.

My life closed twice before its close—

EMILY DICKINSON

My life closed twice before its close—
It yet remains to see
If Immortality unveil
A third event to me

So huge, so hopeless to conceive
As these that twice befell.
Parting is all we know of heaven,
And all we need of hell.

When We Two Parted

GEORGE GORDON, LORD BYRON

When we two parted
   In silence and tears,
Half broken-hearted
   To sever for years,
Pale grew thy cheek and cold,
   Colder thy kiss;
Truly that hour foretold
   Sorrow to this.

The dew of the morning
   Sunk chill on my brow—
It felt like the warning
   Of what I feel now.
Thy vows are all broken,
   And light is thy fame;
I hear thy name spoken,
   And share in its shame.

They name thee before me,
   A knell to mine ear;
A shudder comes o'er me—
   Why wert thou so dear?
They know not I knew thee,
   Who knew thee too well:—
Long, long shall I rue thee,
   Too deeply to tell.

In secret we met—
   In silence I grieve,

That thy heart could forget,
   Thy spirit deceive.
If I should meet thee
   After long years,
How should I greet thee?—
   With silence and tears.

Well, I Have Lost You

EDNA ST. VINCENT MILLAY

Well, I have lost you; and I lost you fairly;
In my own way, and with my full consent.
Say what you will, kings in a tumbrel rarely
Went to their deaths more proud than this one went.
Some nights of apprehension and hot weeping
I will confess; but that's permitted me;
Day dried my eyes; I was not one for keeping
Rubbed in a cage a wing that would be free.
If I had loved you less or played you slyly
I might have held you for a summer more,
But at the cost of words I value highly,
And no such summer as the one before.
Should I outlive this anguish—and men do—
I shall have only good to say of you.

What lips my lips have kissed, and where, and why (Sonnet XLIII)

EDNA ST. VINCENT MILLAY

What lips my lips have kissed, and where, and why,
I have forgotten, and what arms have lain
Under my head till morning; but the rain
Is full of ghosts tonight, that tap and sigh
Upon the glass and listen for reply,
And in my heart there stirs a quiet pain
For unremembered lads that not again
Will turn to me at midnight with a cry.
Thus in winter stands the lonely tree,
Nor knows what birds have vanished one by one,
Yet knows its boughs more silent than before:
I cannot say what loves have come and gone,
I only know that summer sang in me
A little while, that in me sings no more.

"No, Thank You, John"

CHRISTINA ROSSETTI

I never said I loved you, John:
　　Why will you teaze me day by day,
And wax a weariness to think upon
　　With always "do" and "pray"?

You know I never loved you, John;
　　No fault of mine made me your toast:
Why will you haunt me with a face as wan
　　As shows an hour-old ghost?

I dare say Meg or Moll would take
　　Pity upon you, if you'd ask:
And pray don't remain single for my sake
　　Who can't perform that task.

I have no heart?—Perhaps I have not;
　　But then you're mad to take offence
That I don't give you what I have not got:
　　Use your own common sense.

Let bygones be bygones:
　　Don't call me false, who owed not to be true:
I'd rather answer "No" to fifty Johns
　　Than answer "Yes" to you.

Let's mar our pleasant days no more,
　　Song-birds of passage, days of youth:
Catch at today, forget the days before:
　　I'll wink at your untruth.

Let us strike hands as hearty friends;
  No more, no less; and friendship's good:
Only don't keep in view ulterior ends,
  And points not understood

In open treaty. Rise above
  Quibbles and shuffling off and on:
Here's friendship for you if you like; but love,—
  No, thank you, John.

when you have forgotten Sunday: the love story

GWENDOLYN BROOKS

——And when you have forgotten the bright bedclothes
    on a Wednesday and a Saturday,
And most especially when you have forgotten Sunday—
When you have forgotten Sunday halves in bed;
Or me sitting on the front-room radiator in the limping afternoon
Looking off down the long street
To nowhere,
Hugged by my plain old wrapper of no-expectation
And nothing-I-have-to-do and I'm-happy-why?
And if-Monday-never-had-to-come—
When you have forgotten that, I say,
And how you swore, if somebody beeped the bell,
And how my heart played hopscotch if the telephone
    rang;
And how we finally went in to Sunday dinner,
That is to say, went across the front room floor to the
    ink-spotted table in the southwest corner
To Sunday dinner, which was always chicken and
    noodles
Or chicken and rice
And salad and rye bread and tea
And chocolate chip cookies—
I say, when you have forgotten that,
When you have forgotten my little presentiment
That the war would be over before they got to you;
And how we finally undressed and whipped out the light
    and flowed into bed,
And lay loose-limbed for a moment in the week-end

Bright bedclothes,
Then gently folded into each other—
When you have, I say, forgotten all that,
Then you may tell,
Then I may believe
You have forgotten me well.

The End

ELIZABETH ALEXANDER

The last thing of you is a doll, velveteen and spangle,
silk douponi trousers, Ali Baba slippers that curl up at the toes,
tinsel moustache, a doll we had made in your image
for our wedding with one of me which you have.
They sat atop our coconut cake. We cut it
into snowy squares and fed each other, while God watched.

All other things are gone now: the letters boxed,
pajama-sized shirts bagged for Goodwill, odd utensils
farmed to graduating students starting first apartments
(citrus zester, apple corer, rusting mandoline),
childhood pictures returned to your mother,
trinkets sorted real from fake and molten
to a single bar of gold, untruths parsed,
most things unsnarled, the rest let go

save the doll, which I find in a closet,
examine closely, then set into a hospitable tree
which I drive past daily for weeks and see it still there,
in the rain, in the wind, fading in the sun,
no one will take it, it will not blow away,

in the rain, in the wind,

it holds tight to its branch,

then one day, it is gone.

MARRIAGE

GETTING MARRIED WAS THE BEST DECISION I have ever made. Not only is my husband the most wonderful person imaginable, but at the time, it was such a relief to have it all over with! Even though I was a first-year law student determined to concentrate on my professional options, getting married took over my life. To be honest, it had always been a major preoccupation for me, my friends and cousins. We spent countless childhood hours planning imaginary weddings. Would we elope? Could we bring our ponies? What would our bridesmaids wear, especially if they were on their ponies. When I hit my twenties and people started getting married for real, weekends were consumed with bridal showers—complete with skits, songs, and the occasional stripper. There were endless fittings for hideous dresses, but also lots of laughs and backstage drama. My wedding was no exception. Fortunately, I had a fantastic time, and life has only gotten better because I have someone to share it with.

Each marriage is as unique as the two people in it, but universal too. Getting married is an act of hope and optimism—an affirmation of life. Every marriage, like every life, goes through its ups and downs, and the institution of marriage is challenged by personal and historical inequities. Yet the pursuit of love and the strength of a lifelong commitment remain their own rewards and the foundation of much of our social order.

Most of these poems are romantic, realistic, wise, and funny. It's hard not to be swept off one's feet reading Christopher Marlowe's poem "The Passionate Shepherd to His Love." The romantic ideal underlying marriage is embodied by the excerpt from *The Countess of Pembroke's Arcadia* by Sir Philip Sidney. Its most famous line, "My true love hath my heart and I have his," is echoed by e. e. cummings four hundred years later when he writes, "i carry your heart with me(i carry it in/my heart)."

I have tried to include poems that examine different aspects of the marital relationship. Comparing a passage from the Book of Proverbs about the virtuous wife to Lady Mary Chudleigh's warning in "To the Ladies" gives us a historical perspective on the relative status of husbands and wives. Not surprisingly, women come up short. There are also grim, loveless depictions like Robert Lowell's "To Speak of Woe That Is in Marriage." Even more chilling is Robert Browning's classic "My Last Duchess," in which the fact that the husband has murdered his wife is gradually revealed.

At least Ogden Nash and Rudyard Kipling bring a little levity to the subject. In "A Word to Husbands" and "The Female of the Species," they complain loudly that women dominate the home and everyone who enters it. An excerpt from John Milton's *Paradise Lost* takes us back to the beginning of the "vain contest" between husband and wife, which he describes as a struggle that shall have no end.

Fortunately, however, most poems about marriage celebrate companionship, passion, and the oneness of two people in a long-term partnership. "Letter from My Wife" is one of many poems written from prison by Nazim Hikmet, a Turkish poet jailed for his political activities. Filled with longing and the desire to be reunited before death, these poems make the reader's heart ache.

Poet Laureate W. S. Merwin's poem "To Paula in Late Spring" reflects on the memories of a lifetime of love.

Even though each marriage remains unique and mysterious, these poems underscore how and why getting married remains such a powerful personal and societal ideal.

The Passionate Shepherd to His Love

CHRISTOPHER MARLOWE

Come live with me, and be my love,
And we will all the pleasures prove,
That valleys, groves, hills, and fields,
Woods, or steepy mountain yields.

And we will sit upon the rocks,
Seeing the shepherds feed their flocks,
By shallow rivers to whose falls
Melodious birds sing madrigals.

And I will make thee beds of roses,
And a thousand fragrant posies,
A cap of flowers, and a kirtle,
Embroidered all with leaves of myrtle;

A gown made of the finest wool,
Which from our pretty lambs we pull;
Fair lined slippers for the cold,
With buckles of the purest gold;

A belt of straw and ivy buds,
With coral clasps and amber studs:
And if these pleasures may thee move,
Come live with me, and be my love.

The shepherds' swains shall dance and sing
For thy delight each May morning.
If these delights thy mind may move,
Then live with me, and be my love.

Marriage

GREGORY CORSO

Should I get married? Should I be good?
Astound the girl next door with my velvet suit and faustus hood?
Don't take her to movies but to cemeteries
tell all about werewolf bathtubs and forked clarinets
then desire her and kiss her and all the preliminaries
and she going just so far and I understanding why
not getting angry saying You must feel! It's beautiful to feel!
Instead take her in my arms lean against an old crooked
    tombstone
and woo her the entire night the constellations in the sky—

When she introduces me to her parents
back straightened, hair finally combed, strangled by a tie,
should I sit knees together on their 3rd degree sofa
and not ask Where's the bathroom?
How else to feel other than I am,
often thinking Flash Gordon soap—
O how terrible it must be for a young man
seated before a family and the family thinking
We never saw him before! He wants our Mary Lou!
After tea and homemade cookies they ask What do you do for a
    living?

Should I tell them? Would they like me then?
Say All right get married, we're losing a daughter
but we're gaining a son—
And should I then ask Where's the bathroom?
O God, and the wedding! All her family and her friends
and only a handful of mine all scroungy and bearded

just wait to get at the drinks and food—
And the priest! he looking at me as if I masturbated
asking me Do you take this woman for your lawful wedded wife?
And I trembling what to say say Pie Glue!
I kiss the bride all those corny men slapping me on the back
She's all yours, boy! Ha-ha-ha!
And in their eyes you could see some obscene honeymoon going

on—

Then all that absurd rice and clanky cans and shoes
Niagara Falls! Hordes of us! Husbands! Wives! Flowers!

Chocolates!

All streaming into cozy hotels
All going to do the same thing tonight
The indifferent clerk he knowing what was going to happen
The lobby zombies they knowing what
The whistling elevator man he knowing
The winking bellboy knowing
Everybody knowing! I'd be almost inclined not to do anything!
Stay up all night! Stare that hotel clerk in the eye!
Screaming: I deny honeymoon! I deny honeymoon!
running rampant into those almost climactic suites
yelling Radio belly! Cat shovel!
O I'd live in Niagara forever! in a dark cave beneath the Falls
I'd sit there the Mad Honeymooner
devising ways to break marriages, a scourge of bigamy
a saint of divorce—

But I should get married I should be good
How nice it'd be to come home to her
and sit by the fireplace and she in the kitchen
aproned young and lovely wanting my baby
and so happy about me she burns the roast beef
and comes crying to me and I get up from my big papa chair

saying Christmas teeth! Radiant brains! Apple deaf!
God what a husband I'd make! Yes, I should get married!
So much to do! like sneaking into Mr. Jones' house late at night
and cover his golf clubs with 1920 Norwegian books
Like hanging a picture of Rimbaud on the lawnmower
like pasting Tannu Tuva postage stamps all over the picket fence
like when Mrs Kindhead comes to collect for the Community
    Chest
grab her and tell her There are unfavorable omens in the sky!
And when the mayor comes to get my vote tell him
When are you going to stop people killing whales!
And when the milkman comes leave him a note in the bottle
Penguin dust, bring me penguin dust, I want penguin dust—

Yet if I should get married and it's Connecticut and snow
and she gives birth to a child and I am sleepless, worn,
up for nights, head bowed against a quiet window, the past
    behind me,
finding myself in the most common of situations a trembling man
knowledged with responsibility not twig-smear nor Roman coin
                                                    soup—
O what would that be like!
Surely I'd give it for a nipple a rubber Tacitus
For a rattle a bag of broken Bach records
Tack Della Francesca all over its crib
Sew the Greek alphabet on its bib
And build for its playpen a roofless Parthenon

No, I doubt I'd be that kind of father
not rural not snow no quiet window
but hot smelly tight New York City
seven flights up, roaches and rats in the walls
a fat Reichian wife screeching over potatoes Get a job!

And five nose running brats in love with Batman
And the neighbors all toothless and dry haired
like those hag masses of the 18th century
all wanting to come in and watch TV
The landlord wants his rent
Grocery store Blue Cross Gas & Electric Knights of Columbus
Impossible to lie back and dream Telephone snow, ghost parking—
No! I should not get married I should never get married!
But—imagine If I were married to a beautiful sophisticated woman
tall and pale wearing an elegant black dress and long black gloves
holding a cigarette holder in one hand and a highball in the other
and we lived high up in a penthouse with a huge window
from which we could see all of New York and ever farther on
                                            clearer days
No, can't imagine myself married to that pleasant prison dream—

O but what about love? I forget love
not that I am incapable of love
it's just that I see love as odd as wearing shoes—
I never wanted to marry a girl who was like my mother
And Ingrid Bergman was always impossible
And there's maybe a girl now but she's already married
And I don't like men and—
but there's got to be somebody!
Because what if I'm 60 years old and not married,
all alone in a furnished room with pee stains on my underwear
and everybody else is married! All the universe married but me!

Ah, yet well I know that were a woman possible as I am possible
then marriage would be possible—
Like SHE in her lonely alien gaud waiting her Egyptian lover
so I wait—bereft of 2,000 years and the bath of life.

From *The Countess of Pembroke's Arcadia*

SIR PHILIP SIDNEY

My true love hath my heart, and I have his,
By just exchange one for the other given.
I hold his dear, and mine he cannot miss:
There never was a better bargain driven.
His heart in me keeps me and him in one;
My heart in him his thoughts and senses guides;
He loves my heart, for once it was his own;
I cherish his, because in me it bides.
His heart his wound receivèd from my sight;
My heart was wounded with his wounded heart;
For as from me on him his hurt did light,
So still, methought, in me his hurt did smart;
   Both equal hurt, in this change sought our bliss:
   My true love hath my heart, and I have his.

i carry your heart with me(i carry it in

E. E. CUMMINGS

i carry your heart with me(i carry it in
my heart)i am never without it(anywhere
i go you go,my dear;and whatever is done
by only me is your doing,my darling)
                                        i fear
no fate(for you are my fate,my sweet)i want
no world(for beautiful you are my world,my true)
and it's you are whatever a moon has always meant
and whatever a sun will always sing is you

here is the deepest secret nobody knows
(here is the root of the root and the bud of the bud
and the sky of the sky of a tree called life;which grows
higher than soul can hope or mind can hide)
and this is the wonder that's keeping the stars apart

i carry your heart(i carry it in my heart)

To My Dear and Loving Husband

ANNE BRADSTREET

If ever two were one, then surely we.
If ever man were lov'd by wife, then thee;
If ever wife was happy in a man,
Compare with me ye women if you can.
I prize thy love more than whole mines of gold,
Or all the riches that the East doth hold.
My love is such that rivers cannot quench,
Nor aught but love from thee, give recompense.
Thy love is such I can no way repay,
The heavens reward thee manifold, I pray.
Then while we live, in love let's so persever
That, when we live no more, we may live ever.

To Margo

GAVIN EWART

In life's rough-and-tumble
you're the crumble on my apple crumble
and the fairy on my Christmas tree!
In life's death-and-duty
you've the beauty of the Beast's own Beauty—
I feel humble as a bumble-bee!

In life's darkening duel
I'm the lighter, you're the lighter fuel—
and the tide that sways my inland sea!
In life's meet-and-muster
you've the lustre of a diamond cluster—
a blockbuster—just a duster, me!

A Word to Husbands

OGDEN NASH

To keep your marriage brimming,
With love in the loving cup,
Whenever you're wrong, admit it;
Whenever you're right, shut up.

To the Ladies

LADY MARY CHUDLEIGH

Wife and servant are the same,
But only differ in the name:
For when that fatal knot is tied,
Which nothing, nothing can divide:
When she the word *obey* has said,
And man by law supreme has made,
Then all that's kind is laid aside,
And nothing left but state and pride:
Fierce as an Eastern prince he grows,
And all his innate rigour shows:
Then but to look, to laugh, or speak,
Will the nuptial contract break.
Like mutes she signs alone must make,
And never any freedom take:
But still be governed by a nod,
And fear her husband as a God:
Him still must serve, him still obey,
And nothing act, and nothing say,
But what her haughty lord thinks fit,
Who with the power, has all the wit.
Then shun, oh! shun that wretched state,
And all the fawning flatt'rers hate:
Value your selves, and men despise,
You must be proud, if you'll be wise.

The Female of the Species

RUDYARD KIPLING

When the Himalayan peasant meets the he-bear in his pride,
He shouts to scare the monster, who will often turn aside.
But the she-bear thus accosted rends the peasant tooth and nail.
For the female of the species is more deadly than the male.

When Nag the basking cobra hears the careless foot of man,
He will sometimes wriggle sideways and avoid it as he can.
But his mate makes no such motion where she camps beside
    the trail.
For the female of the species is more deadly than the male.

When the early Jesuit fathers preached to Hurons and Choctaws,
They prayed to be delivered from the vengeance of the squaws.
'Twas the women, not the warriors, turned those stark enthusiasts
    pale.
For the female of the species is more deadly than the male.

Man's timid heart is bursting with the things he must not say,
For the Woman that God gave him isn't his to give away;
But when hunter meets with husband, each confirms the other's
    tale—
The female of the species is more deadly than the male.

Man, a bear in most relations—worm and savage otherwise,—
Man propounds negotiations, Man accepts the compromise.
Very rarely will he squarely push the logic of a fact
To its ultimate conclusion in unmitigated act.

Fear, or foolishness, impels him, ere he lay the wicked low,
To concede some form of trial even to his fiercest foe.
Mirth obscene diverts his anger! Doubt and Pity oft perplex
Him in dealing with an issue—to the scandal of The Sex!

But the Woman that God gave him, every fibre of her frame
Proves her launched for one sole issue, armed and engined
     for the same;
And to serve that single issue, lest the generations fail,
The female of the species must be deadlier than the male.

She who faces Death by torture for each life beneath her breast
May not deal in doubt or pity—must not swerve for fact or jest.
These be purely male diversions—not in these her honour dwells.
She the Other Law we live by, is that Law and nothing else.

She can bring no more to living than the powers that make her
     great
As the Mother of the Infant and the Mistress of the Mate!
And when Babe and Man are lacking and she strides unclaimed
     to claim
Her right as femme (and baron), her equipment is the same.

She is wedded to convictions—in default of grosser ties;
Her contentions are her children, Heaven help him who denies!—
He will meet no suave discussion, but the instant, white-hot, wild,
Wakened female of the species warring as for spouse and child.

Unprovoked and awful charges—even so the she-bear fights,
Speech that drips, corrodes and poisons—even so the cobra bites,
Scientific vivisection of one nerve till it is raw
And the victim writhes in anguish—like the Jesuit with the squaw!

So it comes that Man, the coward, when he gathers to confer
With his fellow-braves in council, dare not leave a place for her
Where, at war with Life and Conscience, he uplifts his erring hands
To some God of Abstract Justice—which no woman understands.

And Man knows it! Knows, moreover, that the Woman that God
   gave him
Must command but may not govern—shall enthral but not enslave
   him.
And *She* knows, because She warns him, and Her instincts never
   fail,
That the Female of Her Species is more deadly than the Male.

From *Paradise Lost*

JOHN MILTON

Eve to herself after eating the apple:
> I grow mature
In knowledge, as the gods who all things know;
Though others envy what they cannot give;

. . .

> But to Adam in what sort
Shall I appear? shall I to him make known
As yet my change, and give him to partake
Full happiness with me, or rather not,
But keep the odds of knowledge in my power
Without copartner? so to add what wants
In female sex, the more to draw his love,
And render me more equal, and perhaps,
A thing not undesirable, sometime
Superior; for inferior who is free?
This may be well: but what if God have seen,
And death ensue? then I shall be no more,
And Adam wedded to another Eve,
Shall live with her enjoying, I extinct;
A death to think. Confirmed then I resolve,
Adam shall share with me in bliss or woe:
So dear I love him, that with him all deaths
I could endure, without him live no life.

. . .

Adam to himself after learning that Eve has eaten the apple:
> O fairest of Creation, last and best
Of all God's works, creature in whom excelled
Whatever can to sight or thought be formed,

Holy, divine, good, amiable or sweet!
How art thou lost, how on a sudden lost,
Defaced, deflow'red, and now to death devote?
Rather how hast thou yielded to transgress
The strict forbiddance, how to violate
The sacred fruit forbidd'n! Some cursèd fraud
Of Enemy hath beguiled thee, yet unknown,
And me with thee hath ruined, for with thee
Certain my resolution is to die;
How can I live without thee, how forgo
Thy sweet convérse and love so dearly joined,
To live again in these wild woods forlorn?
Should God create another Eve, and I
Another rib afford, yet loss of thee
Would never from my heart; no no, I feel
The link of nature draw me: flesh of flesh,
Bone of my bone thou art, and from thy state
Mine never shall be parted, bliss or woe.

   . . .

And later on:
Covered, but not at rest or ease of mind,
They sat them down to weep, nor only tears
Rained at their eyes, but high winds worse within
Began to rise, high passions, anger, hate,
Mistrust, suspicion, discord, and shook sore
Their inward state of mind, calm region once
And full of peace, now tossed and turbulent:
For understanding ruled not, and the will
Heard not her lore, both in subjection now
To sensual appetite, who from beneath
Usurping over sov'reign reason claimed
Superior sway: from thus distempered breast,

Adam, estranged in look and altered style,
Speech intermitted thus to Eve renewed.

   Would thou hadst hearkened to my words, and stayed
With me, as I besought thee, when that strange
Desire of wand'ring this unhappy morn,
I know not whence possessed thee; we had then
Remained still happy, not as now, despoiled
Of all our good, shamed, naked, miserable.
Let none henceforth seek needless cause to approve
The faith they owe; when earnestly they seek
Such proof, conclude, they then begin to fail.

   To whom soon moved with touch of blame thus Eve.
What words have passed thy lips, Adam severe,
Imput'st thou that to my default, or will
Of wand'ring, as thou call'st it, which who knows
But might as ill have happened thou being by,
Or to thyself perhaps: hadst thou been there,
Or here th' attempt, thou couldst not have discerned
Fraud in the serpent, speaking as he spake;
No ground of enmity between us known,
Why he should mean me ill, or seek to harm.
Was I to have never parted from thy side?
As good have grown there still a lifeless rib.
Being as I am, why didst not thou the head
Command me absolutely not to go,
Going into such danger as thou saidst?
Too facile then thou didst not much gainsay,
Nay, didst permit, approve, and fair dismiss.
Hadst thou been firm and fixed in thy dissent,
Neither had I transgressed, nor thou with me.

   To whom then first incensed Adam replied.
Is this the love, is this the recompense
Of mine to thee, ingrateful Eve, expressed

Immutable when thou wert lost, not I,
Who might have lived and joyed immortal bliss,
Yet willingly chose rather death with thee:
And am I now upbraided, as the cause
Of thy transgressing? not enough severe,
It seems, in thy restraint: what could I more?
I warned thee, I admonished thee, foretold
The danger, and the lurking Enemy
That lay in wait; beyond this had been force,
And force upon free will hath here no place.
But confidence then bore thee on, secure
Either to meet no danger, or to find
Matter of glorious trial, and perhaps
I also erred in overmuch admiring
What seemed in thee so perfect, that I thought
No evil durst attempt thee, but I rue
That error now, which is become my crime,
And thou th' accuser. Thus it shall befall
Him who to worth in women overtrusting
Lets her will rule; restraint she will not brook,
And left to herself, if evil thence ensue,
She first his weak indulgence will accuse.

   Thus they in mutual accusation spent
The fruitless hours, but neither self-condemning,
And of their vain contést appeared no end.

The Good Wife

PROVERBS 31:10–31

Who can find a virtuous woman?
For her price is far above rubies.

The heart of her husband doth safely trust in her,
So that he shall have no need of spoil.

She will do him good and not evil
All the days of her life.

She seeketh wool and flax,
And worketh willingly with her hands.

She is like the merchants' ships;
She bringeth her food from afar.

She riseth also while it is yet night,
And giveth meat to her household, and a portion to her maidens.

She considereth a field, and buyeth it:
With the fruit of her hands she planteth a vineyard.

She girdeth her loins with strength,
And strengtheneth her arms.

She perceiveth that her merchandise is good:
Her candle goeth not out by night.

She layeth her hands to the spindle,
And her hands hold the distaff.

She stretcheth out her hand to the poor;
Yea, she reacheth forth her hands to the needy.

She is not afraid of the snow for her household:
For all her household are clothed with scarlet.

She maketh herself coverings of tapestry;
Her clothing is silk and purple.

Her husband is known in the gates,
When he sitteth among the elders of the land.

She maketh fine linen, and selleth it;
And delivereth girdles unto the merchant.

Strength and honor are her clothing;
And she shall rejoice in time to come.

She openeth her mouth with wisdom;
And in her tongue is the law of kindness.

She looketh well to the ways of her household,
And eateth not the bread of idleness.

Her children arise up, and call her blessed;
Her husband also, and he praiseth her:

"Many daughters have done virtuously,
But thou excellest them all."

Favor is deceitful, and beauty is vain:
But a woman that feareth the Lord,
She shall be praised.

Give her of the fruit of her hands;
and let her own works praise her in the gates.

My Last Duchess

ROBERT BROWNING

Ferrara:

That's my last Duchess painted on the wall,
Looking as if she were alive. I call
That piece a wonder, now: Frà Pandolf's hands
Worked busily a day, and there she stands.
Will't please you sit and look at her? I said
'Frà Pandolf' by design, for never read
Strangers like you that pictured countenance,
The depth and passion of its earnest glance,
But to myself they turned (since none puts by
The curtain I have drawn for you, but I)
And seemed as they would ask me, if they durst,
How such a glance came there; so, not the first
Are you to turn and ask thus. Sir, 'twas not
Her husband's presence only, called that spot
Of joy into the Duchess' cheek: perhaps
Frà Pandolf chanced to say 'Her mantle laps
Over my lady's wrist too much,' or 'Paint
Must never hope to reproduce the faint
Half-flush that dies along her throat': such stuff
Was courtesy, she thought, and cause enough
For calling up that spot of joy. She had
A heart—how shall I say?—too soon made glad,
Too easily impressed; she liked whate'er
She looked on, and her looks went everywhere.
Sir, 'twas all one! My favour at her breast,
The dropping of the daylight in the West,
The bough of cherries some officious fool
Broke in the orchard for her, the white mule

She rode with round the terrace—all and each
Would draw from her alike the approving speech,
Or blush, at least. She thanked men,—good! but thanked
Somehow—I know not how—as if she ranked
My gift of a nine-hundred-years-old name
With anybody's gift. Who'd stoop to blame
This sort of trifling? Even had you skill
In speech—(which I have not)—to make your will
Quite clear to such an one, and say, 'Just this
Or that in you disgusts me; here you miss,
Or there exceed the mark'—and if she let
Herself be lessoned so, nor plainly set
Her wits to yours, forsooth, and made excuse,
—E'en then would be some stooping; and I choose
Never to stoop. Oh sir, she smiled, no doubt,
Whene'er I passed her; but who passed without
Much the same smile? This grew; I gave commands;
Then all smiles stopped together. There she stands
As if alive. Will't please you rise? We'll meet
The company below, then. I repeat,
The Count your master's known munificence
Is ample warrant that no just pretence
Of mine for dowry will be disallowed;
Though his fair daughter's self, as I avowed
At starting, is my object. Nay, we'll go
Together down, sir. Notice Neptune, though,
Taming a sea-horse, thought a rarity,
Which Claus of Innsbruck cast in bronze for me!

To Speak of Woe That Is in Marriage

ROBERT LOWELL

"It is the future generation that presses into being by means of these
exuberant feelings and super-sensible soap bubbles of ours."

SCHOPENHAUER

"The hot night makes us keep our bedroom windows open.
Our magnolia blossoms. Life begins to happen.
My hopped up husband drops his home disputes,
and hits the streets to cruise for prostitutes,
free-lancing out along the razor's edge.
This screwball might kill his wife, then take the pledge.
Oh the monotonous meanness of his lust ...
It's the injustice ... he is so unjust—
whiskey-blind, swaggering home at five.
My only thought is how to keep alive.
What makes him tick? Each night now I tie
ten dollars and his car key to my thigh. . . .
Gored by the climacteric of his want,
he stalls above me like an elephant."

From a Survivor

ADRIENNE RICH

The pact that we made was the ordinary pact
of men & women in those days

I don't know who we thought we were
that our personalities
could resist the failures of the race

Lucky or unlucky, we didn't know
the race had failures of that order
and that we were going to share them

Like everybody else, we thought of ourselves as special

Your body is as vivid to me
as it ever was: even more

since my feeling for it is clearer:
I know what it could do and could not do

it is no longer
the body of a god
or anything with power over my life

Next year it would have been 20 years
and you are wastefully dead
who might have made the leap
we talked, too late, of making

which I live now
not as a leap
but a succession of brief, amazing movements

each one making possible the next

Letter from My Wife

NAZIM HIKMET

I
want to die before you.
Do you think the one who follows
finds the one who went first?
I don't think so.
It would be best to have me burned
and put in a jar
> over your fireplace.
Make the jar
clear glass,
> so you can watch me inside . . .
You see my sacrifice:
I give up being earth,
I give up being a flower,
> just to stay near you.
And I become dust
to live with you.
Then, when you die,
you can come into my jar
and we'll live there together,
your ashes with mine,
until some dizzy bride
or wayward grandson
tosses us out . . .
But
by then
we'll be
so mixed
together

that even at the dump our atoms
                    will fall side by side.
We'll dive into the earth together.
And if one day a wild flower
finds water and springs up from that piece of earth,
its stem will have
two blooms for sure:
                    one will be you,
                    the other me.

I'm
not about to die yet.
I want to bear another child.
I'm brimming with life.
My blood is hot.
I'm going to live a long, long time—
and with you.
Death doesn't scare me,
I just don't find our funeral arrangements
                    too attractive.
But everything could change
before I die.
Any chance you'll get out of prison soon?
Something inside me says:
                    Maybe.

To Paula in Late Spring

W. S. MERWIN

Let me imagine that we will come again
when we want to and it will be spring
we will be no older than we ever were
the worn griefs will have eased like the early cloud
through which the morning slowly comes to itself
and the ancient defenses against the dead
will be done with and left to the dead at last
the light will be as it is now in the garden
that we have made here these years together
of our long evenings and astonishment

A Farmer's Calendar

VIETNAMESE FOLK POEM

The twelfth moon for potato growing,
the first for beans, the second for eggplant.
In the third, we break the land
to plant rice in the fourth while the rains are strong.
The man ploughs, the woman plants,
and in the fifth: the harvest, and the gods are good—
an acre yields five full baskets this year.
I grind and pound the paddy, strew husks to cover the manure,
and feed the hogs with bran.
Next year, if the land is extravagant,
I shall pay the taxes for you.
In plenty or in want, there will still be you and me,
always the two of us.
Isn't that better than always prospering, alone?

LOVE ITSELF

L OVE POETRY IS the greatest poetry in the English language. Women have always been at its center. We are its inspiration, we are its readers, and increasingly, women are its authors. And how many men like to read poetry anyway?

It's hard to say anything new about something as all-encompassing, as infinite, complex, and mysterious, as intricate and detailed, as abstract and powerful as love. Many of these poems will be familiar. The most famous among them have entered our subconscious and help define how our society thinks about love. Less well-known poems bring new insight and metaphor. There are a few things more pleasurable than reading love poetry. I think you can guess what they are, but until then, I hope you enjoy reading these poems as much as I do.

A Birthday

CHRISTINA ROSSETTI

My heart is like a singing bird
   Whose nest is in a watered shoot;
My heart is like an appletree
   Whose boughs are bent with thickset fruit;
My heart is like a rainbow shell
   That paddles in a halcyon sea;
My heart is gladder than all these
   Because my love is come to me.

Raise me a dais of silk and down;
   Hang it with vair and purple dyes;
Carve it in doves, and pomegranates,
   And peacocks with a hundred eyes;
Work it in gold and silver grapes,
   In leaves, and silver fleurs-de-lys;
Because the birthday of my life
   Is come, my love is come to me.

June Light

RICHARD WILBUR

Your voice, with clear location of June days,
Called me—outside the window. You were there,
Light yet composed, as in the just soft stare
Of uncontested summer all things raise
Plainly their seeming into seamless air.

Then your love looked as simple and entire
As that picked pear you tossed me, and your face
As legible as pearskin's fleck and trace,
Which promise always wine, by mottled fire
More fatal fleshed than ever human grace.

And your gay gift—Oh when I saw it fall
Into my hands, through all that naïve light,
It seemed as blessed with truth and new delight
As must have been the first great gift of all.

Protocols

VIKRAM SETH

What can I say to you? How can I now retract
    All that that fool, my voice, has spoken—
Now that the facts are plain, the placid surface cracked,
    The protocols of friendship broken?

I cannot walk by day as now I walk at dawn
    Past the still house where you lie sleeping.
May the sun burn away these footprints on the lawn
    And hold you in its warmth and keeping.

Jamesian

THOM GUNN

Their relationship consisted
In discussing if it existed.

From *Proverbs and Song Verse*

ANTONIO MACHADO

The language of love
was never the worse
for some overstatement.

Sonnet XLIII: How Do I Love Thee?

ELIZABETH BARRETT BROWNING

How do I love thee? Let me count the ways.
I love thee to the depth and breadth and height
My soul can reach, when feeling out of sight
For the ends of Being and ideal Grace.
I love thee to the level of every day's
Most quiet need, by sun and candlelight.
I love thee freely, as men strive for Right;
I love thee purely, as they turn from Praise.
I love thee with the passion put to use
In my old griefs, and with my childhood's faith.
I love thee with a love I seemed to lose
With my lost saints,—I love thee with the breath,
Smiles, tears, of all my life!—and if God choose,
I shall but love thee better after death.

XLIV: You must know that I do not love and *that I love you*

PABLO NERUDA

You must know that I do not love *and* that I love you,
because everything alive has its two sides;
a word is one wing of the silence,
fire has its cold half.

I love you in order to begin to love you,
to start infinity again
and never to stop loving you:
that's why I do not love you yet.

I love you, and I do not love you, as if I held
keys in my hand: to a future of joy—
a wretched, muddled fate—

My love has two lives, in order to love you:
that's why I love you when I do not love you,
and also why I love you when I do.

Code Poem for the French Resistance

LEO MARKS

The life that I have is all that I have,
And the life that I have is yours.
The love that I have of the life that I have
Is yours and yours and yours.

A sleep I shall have
A rest I shall have,
Yet death will be but a pause,
For the peace of my years in the long green grass
Will be yours and yours and yours.

The Smaller Orchid

AMY CLAMPITT

Love is a climate
small things find safe
to grow in—not
(though I once supposed so)
the demanding cattleya
du côté de chez Swann,
glamor among the faubourgs,
hothouse overpowerings, blisses
and cruelties at teatime, but this
next-to-unidentifiable wildling,
hardly more than a
sprout, I've found
flourishing in the hollows
of a granite seashore—
a cheerful tousle, little,
white, down-to-earth orchid
declaring its authenticity,
if you hug the ground
close enough, in a powerful
outdoorsy-domestic
whiff of vanilla.

Sonnet 116

WILLIAM SHAKESPEARE

Let me not to the marriage of true minds
Admit impediments. Love is not love
Which alters when it alteration finds,
Or bends with the remover to remove:
Oh no, it is an ever fixèd mark
That looks on tempests and is never shaken;
It is the star to every wandering bark,
Whose worth's unknown, although his height be taken.
Love's not Time's fool, though rosy lips and cheeks
Within his bending sickle's compass come;
Love alters not with his brief hours and weeks,
But bears it out even to the edge of doom.
   If this be error and upon me proved,
   I never writ, nor no man ever loved.

Out beyond ideas of wrongdoing

RUMI

Out beyond ideas of wrongdoing and rightdoing,
there is a field. I'll meet you there.

When the soul lies down in that grass,
the world is too full to talk about.
Ideas, language, even the phrase *each other*
doesn't make any sense.

The Emperor

MATTHEW ROHRER

She sends me a text
she's coming home
the train emerges
from underground

I light the fire under
the pot, I pour her
a glass of wine
I fold a napkin under
a little fork

the wind blows the rain
into the windows
the emperor himself
is not this happy

Late Fragment

RAYMOND CARVER

And did you get what
you wanted from this life, even so?
I did.
And what did you want?
To call myself beloved, to feel myself
beloved on the earth.

From *The First Morning of the Second World*

DELMORE SCHWARTZ

… Quickly then and certainly it was the river of summer, blue as the
  infinite curving blueness above us,
Little boats at anchor lolled or were lapped, and a yacht slowly
  glided.
It was wholly holiday, holiday absolute, a silk and saraband day,
  warm and gay and
Blue and white and vibrant as the pennants buoyant on the stadium
  near us,
White, a milk whiteness, and also all the colors flaring, melting, or
  flowing.
There hope was, and the hopes, and the years past,
The beings I had known and forgotten and half-remembered or
  remembered too often,
Some in rowboats sunned, as on a picnic, or waiting, as before
  a play,
    the picnic and *the* play of eternity as summer, siesta, and summit
—How could I have known that the years and the hopes were
  human beings hated or loved,
Or known that I knew less and more than I supposed I supposed?
(So I questioned myself, in a voice familiar and strange.)
There they were, all of them, and I was with them,
They were with me, and they were me, I was them, forever united
As we all moved forward in a consonance silent and moving
    Seated and gazing,
      Upon the beautiful river forever.

2

So we were as children on the painted wooden horses, rising and
  falling, of the carnival's carousel

Singing or smiling, at times, as the lyric of a small music tinkled
     above us
Saying: "The task is the round, the round is the task, the task and
     the round are a dance, and
There is nothing to think but drink of love and knowledge, and
     love's knowledge
When after and before are no more, and no more masks or un-
     masking,
          but only basking
(As the shining sea basks under the shining sun
In a radiance of swords and chandeliers dancing)
In the last love of knowledge, the first, when thought's abdication
     quickens thought's exaltation,
In the last blessing and sunlight of love's knowledge."

I hardly knew when my lips parted. Started to move slowly
As in the rehearsal of half-remembered memorized
          anthem, prayer, or spell
               of heartwelling gratitude and recognition.

My lips trembled, fumbled, and in the depths and death of thought
A murmur rose like the hidden humming of summer, when June
     sleeps
In the radiant entrancings of warm light and green security.
Fumbling, feeling for what I had long supposed I had grasped and
          cast aside as worthless,
               the sparks or glitters of pleasure, trivial and transient.

—The phrases like faces came, lucid and vivid, separate, united,
     sincere as pain
With the unity of meaning and emotion long lost, disbelieved or
     denied,
As I sought with the words I had known a candid translation.

So I said then, in a language intimate and half-understood:
"I did not know ... and I knew ... surely I once knew ...
    I must have known ...
Surely sometimes guessed at or suspected,
Knew and did not know what love is,
The measure of pleasure, heart of joy, the light and the heart of
  the light
Which makes all pleasure, joy and love come to be
As light alone gives all colors being, the measure and the treasure
Of the light which unites and distinguishes the bondage and
  freedom in unity and distinction
Which is love ... Love? ... Is love? What is love?"

Suddenly and certainly I saw how surely the measure and
  treasure of pleasure is being as being with, belonging
Figured and touched in the experience of voices in chorus.
      Withness is ripeness,
      Ripeness is withness,
      To be is to be in love,
         Love is the fullness of being.

. . .

If I speak in the tongues of men and of angels, but have not love,
   I am only a resounding gong or a clanging cymbal.
If I have the gift of prophecy and can fathom all mysteries and all
   knowledge, and if I have a faith that can move mountains,
   but have not love, I am nothing.
If I give all I possess to the poor and surrender my body to the
   flames, but have not love, I gain nothing.

Love is patient, love is kind. It does not envy, it does not boast,
   it is not proud.
It is not rude, it is not self-seeking, it is not easily angered,
   it keeps no record of wrongs.
Love does not delight in evil but rejoices with the truth.
It always protects, always trusts, always hopes, always perseveres.

Love never fails. But where there are prophecies, they will cease;
   where there are tongues, they will be stilled; where there is
   knowledge, it will pass away.
For we know in part and we prophesy in part, but when perfec-
   tion comes, the imperfect disappears.
When I was a child, I talked like a child, I thought like a child,
   I reasoned like a child. When I became a man, I put childish
   ways behind me.
Now we see but a poor reflection as in a mirror; then we shall
   see face to face. Now I know in part; then I shall know fully,
   even as I am fully known.

And now these three remain: faith, hope and love. But the
   greatest of these is love.

WORK

I GREW UP IN A TIME when mothers, including my own, went back to work after they had raised their children. My mother had a job before she was married, but not a career. That was for my generation. In the past thirty years, women have become defined by what we do, as well as by whom we love. Now, for the first time, women constitute half the American workforce. At the higher end of the socioeconomic scale, the debate tends to focus on choices and the hidden truth that women without children can advance farther and more easily in the professional world, while for families in the lower half of the income ladder, women are the primary breadwinners in a majority of households and often struggle to support a family alone. For all of us, the challenge is how to balance work and family and do a decent job at both. It's not easy in our society, which gives little support to mothers, still pays women 25 percent less than men for the same job, only grudgingly acknowledges that women still do the majority of housework, parenting, and caregiving, and does a woefully inadequate job of educating our children.

In traditional societies, women were responsible for farming, cooking, weaving, and sewing. Later they became domestic servants, teachers, nurses, and waitresses. In modern times, women are also scientists, lawyers, professors, and poets. So it makes

sense that the world of work has become a subject for women's poetry.

Women poets are often crusaders for social justice and equality. Tillie Olsen went to jail for trying to organize workers in the meat-packing house where she was employed. In the poem "I Want You Women Up North to Know," she writes about the terrible conditions of Texas garment workers. In "PS Education," Ellen Hagan, who teaches poetry in some of New York City's most challenging schools, writes with moral indignation about the ways in which today's educational system is failing our children.

Some kinds of work connect women of many generations. In "Lineage," Margaret Walker writes about her grandmothers who struggled to survive in the harsh and unforgiving world of subsistence farming, but whose strength and joy inspired their granddaughter. Poems about the modern professional workplace are surprisingly hard to find. We can only hope that more poets will shine a light on its benefits and shortcomings, and help us to integrate work more easily into other parts of our lives.

weaponed woman

GWENDOLYN BROOKS

Well, life has been a baffled vehicle
And baffling. But she fights, and
Has fought, according to her lights and
The lenience of her whirling-place.

She fights with semi-folded arms,
Her strong bag, and the stiff
Frost of her face (that challenges "When" and "If.")
And altogether she does Rather Well.

Night Waitress
LYNDA HULL

Reflected in the plate glass, the pies
look like clouds drifting off my shoulder.
I'm telling myself my face has character,
not beauty. It's my mother's Slavic face.
She washed the floor on hands and knees
below the Black Madonna, praying
to her god of sorrows and visions
who's not here tonight when I lay out the plates,
small planets, the cups and moons of saucers.
At this hour the men all look
as if they'd never had mothers.
They do not see me. I bring the cups.
I bring the silver. There's the man
who leans over the jukebox nightly
pressing the combinations
of numbers. I would not stop him
if he touched me, but it's only songs
of risky love he leans into. The cook sings
with the jukebox, a moan and sizzle
into the grill. On his forehead
a tattooed cross furrows,
diminished when he frowns. He sings words
dragged up from the bottom of his lungs.
I want a song that rolls
through the night like a big Cadillac
past factories to the refineries
squatting on the bay, round and shiny
as the coffee urn warming my palm.
Sometimes when coffee cruises my mind

visiting the most remote way stations,
I think of my room as a calm arrival
each book and lamp in its place. The calendar
on my wall predicts no disaster
only another white square waiting
to be filled like the desire that fills
jail cells, the old arrest
that makes me stare out the window or want
to try every bar down the street.
When I walk out of here in the morning
my mouth is bitter with sleeplessness.
Men surge to the factories and I'm too tired
to look. Fingers grip lunch box handles,
belt buckles gleam, wind riffles my uniform
and it's not romantic when the sun unlids
the end of the avenue. I'm fading
in the morning's insinuations
collecting in the crevices of buildings,
in wrinkles, in every fault
of this frail machinery.

In an Iridescent Time

RUTH STONE

My mother, when young, scrubbed laundry in a tub,
She and her sisters on an old brick walk
Under the apple trees, sweet rub-a-dub.
The bees came round their heads, the wrens made talk.
Four young ladies each with a rainbow board
Honed their knuckles, wrung their wrists to red,
Tossed back their braids and wiped their aprons wet.
The Jersey calf beyond the back fence roared;
And all the soft day, swarms about their pet
Buzzed at his big brown eyes and bullish head.
Four times they rinsed, they said. Some things they starched,
Then shook them from the baskets two by two,
And pinned the fluttering intimacies of life
Between the lilac bushes and the yew:
Brown gingham, pink, and skirts of Alice blue.

Madam and Her Madam

LANGSTON HUGHES

I worked for a woman,
She wasn't mean—
But she had a twelve-room
House to clean.

Had to get breakfast,
Dinner, and supper, too—
Then take care of her children
When I got through.

Wash, iron, and scrub,
Walk the dog around—
It was too much,
Nearly broke me down.

I said, Madam,
Can it be
You trying to make a
Pack-horse out of me?

She opened her mouth.
She cried, Oh, no!
You know, Alberta,
I love you so!

I said, Madam,
That may be true—
But I'll be dogged
If I love you!

Letters from Storyville

NATASHA TRETHEWEY

December 1910

Miss Constance Wright
I Schoolhouse Road
Oakvale, Mississippi

My Dearest Constance,

I am not out-of-doors as you feared,
and though I've had to tuck the blue, wool suit
you gave me, I do now have plenty to eat.
I have no doubt my decision will cause you
much distress, but still I must tell you—
when I had grown too weary to keep up
my inquiries and my rent was coming
due, I had what must be considered
the good fortune to meet Countess P—,
an elegant businesswoman who offered
me a place in her house. I did not accept
then, though I had tea with her—the first
I'd had in days. And later, too hungry
to reason, I spent the last of my purse
on a good meal. It was to her that I went
when I had to leave my hotel, and I am
as yet adjusting to my new life.

This first week I sat—as required—
each evening in the parlor, unnoticed,
the "professor" working the piano

into a frenzy, a single cockroach
scaling the flocked-velvet wallpaper.
The men who've come have called only
on the girls they know—their laughter
trailing off behind them, their gowns
floating past the balustrade. Though
she's said nothing, Countess is indeed
sympathetic. Just the other night
she introduced me to a longtime client
in hopes that he'd take a liking to me.
I was too shy to speak and only pretended
to sip the wine he'd ordered. Of course,
he found me dull and soon excused himself
to find another girl. Part of me was
quite relieved, though I knew I could not
earn a living that way.

                 And so, last night
I was auctioned as a newcomer
to the house—as yet untouched, though
Countess knows well the thing from which
I've run. Many of the girls do too,
and some of them even speak of a child
they left behind. The auction was a near
quiet affair—much like the one Whitman
described, the men some wealthy "gentlemen"
from out of town. Countess announced
that I recite poetry, hinting at a more dignified
birth and thus a tragic occasion for my arrival
at her house. She calls me *Violet* now—
a common name here in Storyville—except
that I am the *African Violet* for the promise
of that wild continent hidden beneath

my white skin. At her cue, I walked slowly
across the room, paused in strange postures
until she called out, *Tableau vivant,* and
I could again move—all this to show
the musical undulation of my hips, my grace,
and my patience which was to mean
that it is my nature to please and that I could,
if so desired, pose still as a statue for hours,
a glass or a pair of boots propped upon my back.

And then, in my borrowed gown
I went upstairs with the highest bidder.
He did not know to call me

Ophelia

Lineage

MARGARET WALKER

My grandmothers were strong.
They followed plows and bent to toil.
They moved through fields sowing seed.
They touched earth and grain grew.
They were full of sturdiness and singing.
My grandmothers were strong.

My grandmothers are full of memories
Smelling of soap and onions and wet clay
With veins rolling roughly over quick hands
They have many clean words to say.
My grandmothers were strong.
Why am I not as they?

I Want You Women Up North to Know

TILLIE OLSEN

(Based on a Letter by Felipe Ibarro in New Masses, Jan. 9th, 1934)

i want you women up north to know
how those dainty children's dresses you buy
    at macy's, wanamakers, gimbels, marshall fields,
are dyed in blood, are stitched in wasting flesh,
down in San Antonio, "where sunshine spends the winter."

I want you women up north to see
the obsequious smile, the salesladies trill
    "exquisite work, madame, exquisite pleats"
vanish into a bloated face, ordering more dresses,
    gouging the wages down,
dissolve into maria, ambrosa, catalina,
    stitching these dresses from dawn to night,
    in blood, in wasting flesh.

Catalina Rodriguez, 24,
    body shriveled to a child's at twelve,
catalina rodriguez, last stages of consumption,
    works for three dollars a week from dawn to midnight.
A fog of pain thickens over her skull, the parching heat
    breaks over her body,
and the bright red blood embroiders the floor of her room.
    White rain stitching the night, the bourgeois poet would say,
    white gulls of hands, darting, veering,
    white lightning, threading the clouds,
this is the exquisite dance of her hands over the cloth,
    and her cough, gay, quick, staccato,

like skeleton's bones clattering,
is appropriate accompaniment for the esthetic dance
    of her fingers,
and the tremolo, tremolo when the hands tremble with pain.
Three dollars a week,
two fifty-five,
seventy cents a week,
no wonder two thousand eight hundred ladies of joy
are spending the winter with the sun after he goes down—
for five cents (who said this was a rich man's world?) you can
    get all the lovin you want
"clap and syph aint much worse than sore fingers, blind eyes, and
    t.m."

Maria Vasquez, spinster,
    for fifteen cents a dozen stitches garments for children she has
    never had,
Catalina Torres, mother of four,
    to keep the starved body starving, embroiders from dawn to
    night.
Mother of four, what does she think of,
    as the needle pocked fingers shift over the silk—
    of the stubble-coarse rags that stretch on her own brood,
    and jut with the bony ridge that marks hunger's landscape
    of fat little prairie-roll bodies that will bulge in the
    silk she needles?
(Be not envious, Catalina Torres, look!
    on your own children's clothing, embroidery,
    more intricate than any a thousand hands could fashion,
    there where the cloth is raveled, or darned,
    designs, multitudinous, complex and handmade by Poverty
    herself.)

Ambrosa Espinoza trusts in god,
   "Todos es de dios, everything is from god,"
    through the dwindling night, the waxing day, she bolsters herself
    up with it—
but the pennies to keep god incarnate, from ambrosa,
and the pennies to keep the priest in wine, from ambrosa,
ambrosa clothes god and priest with hand-made children's dresses.
Her brother lies on an iron cot, all day and watches,
on a mattress of rags he lies.
For twenty-five years he worked for the railroad, then they laid him off
   (racked days, searching for work; rebuffs; suspicious eyes of
     policemen.)
   goodbye ambrosa, mebbe in dallas I find work; desperate swing
    for a freight,
   surprised hands, clutching air, and the wheel goes over a
   leg,
the railroad cuts it off, as it cut off twenty-five years of his life.)
She says that he prays and dreams of another world, as he lies
   there, a heaven (which he does not know was brought to earth
   in 1917 in Russia, by workers like him).

Women up north, I want you to know
when you finger the exquisite handmade dresses
what it means, this working from dawn to midnight,
on what strange feet the feverish dawn must come
   to maria, catalina, ambrosa,
how the malignant fingers twitching over the pallid faces jerk them
    to work,
and the sun and the fever mounts with the day—
   long plodding hours, the eyes burn like coals, heat jellies the
    flying fingers,
down comes the night like blindness.

long hours more with the dim eye of the lamp, the breaking
      back,
   weariness crawls in the flesh like worms, gigantic like earth's in
      winter.
And for Catalina Rodriguez comes the night sweat and the blood
   embroidering the darkness.
   for Catalina Torres the pinched faces of four huddled
   children,
   the naked bodies of four bony children,
   the chant of their chorale of hunger.
And for twenty eight hundred ladies of joy the grotesque act gone
      over—
   the wink—the grimace—the "feeling like it baby?"
And for Maria Vasquez, spinster, emptiness, emptiness,
   flaming with dresses for children she can never fondle.
And for Ambrosa Espinoza—the skeleton body of her brother on
      his mattress
of rags, boring twin holes in the dark with his eyes to the image of
      christ
remembering a leg, and twenty-five years cut off from his life by
      the railroad.

Women up north, I want you to know,
I tell you this can't last forever.

I swear it won't.

PS Education

ELLEN HAGAN

Take all the metal detectors apart and build imaginary cities with them. Then my 7th graders can build a utopia and walk around in it. Tell Harold, the security guard, who sings only Tito Puente songs, that he can have his own music room, and buy gold trumpets and trombones that slide like hot oil. Buy drums that rumble the whole school: da-dum, da-dum. Build a garden as big as the football field at Taft High School and feed everything. Tell Myles he can have a quiet room to fall asleep in, because I know he is tired. I know you are tired, Myles, but you cannot keep calling Russell a fat fuck, "Yo Russell, you fat fuck," over and over until Russell has to stand up and punch Myles where he deserves it most. And why not? Call Russell a genius, who sure knows how to write about his grandma and the shiny wheelchair she rolls in. Tell Shelquan to get down from the air conditioner. He is singing, "This is why I'm hot," with sunglasses he stole from Crystal, whose best friend Kiara has carved the word HATE in her arm. Remind Crystal and her girl Kiara that a woman should never mark her body with a word meant to destroy. Yell at them loudly and when Crystal's nana shows up at the school, tell her anyway, even though she does not speak English and Crystal might not translate. She might. Tell Yaneira that she is a hot skillet when she writes, and not a "retard," which is what Eduardo calls her under his breath. A fire woman. Really. And when Fatumata stops you in the street in front of the McDonald's to say good morning, tell her she is late again, but yes, good morning. And tell her to get out of 339, or ask her to help you make it better. You know she can. Listen to Racheal's poem over and over again. She needs it when Angel, who you cannot believe has turned on you, makes fun of the lilt in her voice, stare him down with your witchy eyes. Tell him, teach him how to say, "I will look at you Racheal and I will see you," 1,000 times over. Racheal, where Trinidad and Guyana meet. Tell her the truth, that you never knew where she was from until you asked, and when you finally asked it was way later than you wanted. Put the principal in class with all the run-down teachers, no pencils, paperless notebooks. Don't give him books because you know he is lazy. Call him lazy. Because he is. Make him walk in and out of the metal detectors, saying, "Next school year I will do better, and serve you better." Make him mean it. Show up. Pencils and papers at the ready.

At the Café

PATRICIA KIRKPATRICK

after Adelia Prado

I must look like I'm confident,
white cup for tea on the table before me,
my son in his indigo bunting,
asleep in the stroller.
When I take out my pen
I must look like a woman
who knows what her work is
while citron and currant
bake in ovens behind me.
Newspaper, lily—
I read in the book that poetry is about the divine.
God came to the window while I was in labor.
Tenderness, tenderness!
I have never forgotten that
sparrow among the clay tiles.
Who knows my name knows I mash
oatmeal, change diapers,
want truly to enter divinity.
God knows it too, knows that
wherever I go now I leave out
some part of me.
I watch my son's face like a clock;
he is the time I have.
If I choose this window, this black-and-white notebook,
I must appear to be what I am:
a woman who has chosen a table
between her sleeping child
and the beginning of everything.

Worked Late on a Tuesday Night

DEBORAH GARRISON

Again.
Midtown is blasted out and silent,
drained of the crowd and its doggy day.
I trample the scraps of deli lunches
some ate outdoors as they stared dumbly
or hooted at us career girls—the haggard
beauties, the vivid can-dos, open raincoats aflap
in the March wind as we crossed to and fro
in front of the Public Library.

Never thought you'd be one of them,
did you, little lady?
Little Miss Phi Beta Kappa,
with your closetful of pleated
skirts, twenty-nine till death do us
part! Don't you see?
The good schoolgirl turns thirty,
forty, singing the song of time management
all day long, lugging the briefcase

home. So at 10:00 PM
you're standing here
with your hand in the air,
cold but too stubborn to reach
into your pocket for a glove, cursing
the freezing rain as though it were
your difficulty. It's pathetic,
and nobody's fault but
your own. Now

the tears,
down into the collar.
Cabs, cabs, but none for hire.
I haven't had dinner; I'm not half
of what I meant to be.
Among other things, the mother
of three. Too tired, tonight,
to seduce the father.

The Age of Great Vocations

ALANE ROLLINGS

You've seen the skirts go up and down
In bread lines, soup lines, cheese lines, shanty towns.
   No one can say you aren't seeking work.
The answers come by mail at noon: No interview.
The best companies never respond; you respect them.
Some days, you don't bother to open the letters,
Just tear them to bits and go out for a walk.
   It's a small fraud by the world's standard:
You can't do things like ask for directions,
So you call yourself an adventure-collector.
Failure's a field with real opportunities
For a girl with a pile of business magazines
Which she will probably have to burn for heat.
Your luck will get either worse or better.
   The world is none of your business;
It doesn't give you a living.

   Someone calls your bluff, asks for references.
You read up on yourself in the library.
With lies, you can double your existence.
   In an endless dream of introductory letters,
The applicants sit in all their best clothes,
Their ages against them, their loneliness
Repeated many times. The managers walk around, choosing.
You say you've done singing telegrams and balloon bouquets
(you've done strip-o-grams, sold flowers at traffic lights).
You're a cake decorator, you've been to zoo school
(you're a weeper-at-weddings, you eat cat food).
Welcome to the world of captivity.

You were calm yesterday, and today you're thinking,
"In the days when I was calm." You'd like
To talk about your sex life. Singing your salesman's song,
You wave your thirteen letters "To Whom It May Concern,"
Every one a masterpiece.
Fooling a man is a full-time job.

You've had a good day? You've found something?
The world needs you right away.
   The loneliness repeats itself.
You chart the progress of your fellow novices
Who stand around as astonished as slaves
Delivered in a day. They aren't moving up,
But they're saying "You bet."
They call the boss The Enemy.

Whatever makes every beginning a sad one
Suggests that somewhere there is something else for you.
Your boss is a terrorist; you like him.
Reading the impressions on his note pad,
You can't help certain hopes.
   Sitting in the switchboard glow,
Connected by the movements of your hands and arms,
You're a shaky presence among solid things.
You don't get a glimpse of his heart of gold,
But you hear things he'd never tell anyone:
He spent his youth dreaming of being a thief;
He is where others ought to be;
People should be ashamed of their luck and proud of their trouble.

At noon you sneak out and eat a stale moon pie
From a filling-station jar. You take gloves to the tramps
Who stand around trash-can fires thanking God

They aren't tramps. You shake their hands.
  The job is impossible, but the enemy,
Meaning your heart, is calm.
That typewriter has not got his eyes or arms:
If you accept its offer, it won't embrace you, yet it offers
Itself more than he does. It won't mind
If you fall asleep in a rush at your desk
Repeating to yourself, "I am asleep," or that
you can't tell in this atmosphere
The difference between sweat and tears.

  You know what all the world knows: time was invented
So workdays could come to a close.
  The women on the electric train
Shift their weight in the direction of the men.
The men stare off, every one for himself,
Every departure a sad one.
  You're not the same person they regarded impatiently
Over the pencil sharpener: you've escaped.
You have to lean against the window frame and laugh.
Cherishing bits of evidence of how strange you are,
You pass through glowing rectangles of town and country.
You think of knights, town criers, jesters.
You can see the world in the last light
Laid out like a checkerboard, and you can live.
  So you're an agent, adjuster, accommodator
With a wish to take the movements of your arms elsewhere.

  Have faith in your doubts.
Your vocation is to feel
Less despair about despair.

  You'll be there until you leave.

Defining Worlds

G. Y. BAXTER

Some would say I chose work
They don't know—it may have chosen me

I'm a working mother
A woman named Sally
Takes care of my baby

Tiny and confused
I can't stay to help

Happy, in fragments
Fleeting, stolen leisure . . .
That time we all paused
To celebrate
A broken BlackBerry

And hectic mornings
And sick days
And school plays
And school's out
And staying late

Running
Running between two worlds

Passing
Passing years
Tears enough to drown me
But I swim

Because mommy must be strong
To live the lesson

I chose to teach her
How to define herself

And she
Letting slide
The forgotten holiday concert
The endless conference call
She is already strong

First with elaborate drawings
in bright markers
Determined, she scribbles
She is proud of me

Then one day
The greeting-card moment
She wants to be just like her mother
And I wonder
Who wouldn't choose that?

What's That Smell in the Kitchen?

MARGE PIERCY

All over America women are burning dinners.
It's lambchops in Peoria; it's haddock
in Providence; it's steak in Chicago
tofu delight in Big Sur; red
rice and beans in Dallas.
All over America women are burning
food they're supposed to bring with calico
smile on platters glittering like wax.
Anger sputters in her brainpan, confined
but spewing out missiles of hot fat.
Carbonized despair presses like a clinker
from a barbecue against the back of her eyes.
If she wants to grill anything, it's
her husband spitted over a slow fire.
If she wants to serve him anything
it's a dead rat with a bomb in its belly
ticking like the heart of an insomniac.
Her life is cooked and digested,
nothing but leftovers in Tupperware.
Look, she says, once I was roast duck
on your platter with parsley but now I am Spam.
Burning dinner is not incompetence but war.

Father Grumble

FOLK SONG

There was an old man who lived in the wood
As you can plainly see,
Who said he could do more work in one day
Than his wife could do in three.

"If this be true," the old woman said,
"Why, this you must allow:
You must do my work for one day
While I go drive the plow.

"And you must milk the Tiny cow
For fear she will go dry,
And you must feed the little pigs
That are within the sty.

"And you must watch the speckled hen
Lest she should lay astray,
And you must wind the reel of yarn
That I spun yesterday."

The old woman took the staff in her hand
And went to drive the plow,
The old man took the pail in his hand
And went to milk the cow.

But Tiny hitched and Tiny flitched,
And Tiny cocked her nose,
And Tiny gave the old man such a kick
That the blood ran down to his hose.

It's "Hey, my good cow!" and "Ho, my good cow!"
And, "Now, my good cow, stand still!
If ever I milk this cow again,
'Twill be against my will."

But Tiny hitched and Tiny flitched,
And Tiny cocked her nose,
And Tiny gave the old man such a kick
That the blood ran down to his hose.

And when he had milked the Tiny cow
For fear she would go dry,
Why then he fed the little pigs
That are within the sty.

And then he watched the speckled hen
Lest she should lay astray,
But he forgot the reel of yarn
His wife spun yesterday.

He swore by all the stars in the sky
And all the leaves on the tree
His wife could do more work in one day
Than he could do in three.

He swore by all the leaves on the tree
And all the stars in heaven
That his wife could do more work in one day
Than he could do in seven.

Epitaph

ANONYMOUS

(Said to have been once found in Bushey Churchyard, Hertfordshire)

Here lies a poor woman who always was tired,
For she lived in a place where help wasn't hired,
Her last words on earth were, "Dear friends, I am going,
Where washing ain't done nor cooking nor sewing,
And everything there is exact to my wishes,
For there they don't eat, there's no washing of dishes,
I'll be where loud anthems will always be ringing
(But having no voice, I'll be out of the singing).
Don't mourn for me now, don't grieve for me never,
For I'm going to do nothing for ever and ever."

BEAUTY, CLOTHES,
AND THINGS
OF THIS WORLD

Y GRANDMOTHERS were the most correct and elegant women I have ever known. They always wore lipstick and perfume, they carried a handbag, even around the house, and they always dressed for dinner. Although they never broke a sweat, they were also athletic and adventurous. They were both coquettes.

My mother became famous for creating her own style, but she learned a lot from her mother. She admired her mother's sense of self-discipline and understatement, but ever since they fought about her wedding dress, she steered my grandmother's critical comments away from her appearance, and toward the length of my brother's hair, the social deterioration of fashion in general, and my summer wardrobe in particular.

On my father's side, none of my aunts took after their fashionable mother—they preferred to dress like their brothers. So my grandmother took an interest in what her granddaughters were wearing instead. She loved dressing up in the same Lilly Pulitzer shift as my cousin Kathleen, and she always told us how important

it was to keep your figure no matter how many children you had. She was proud that she had worn the same dress to meet the King of England in 1939 and to my father's Inaugural Ball in 1960. She taught us to stand sideways with our elbows out when we were being photographed, so as to show off our waists. She had her work cut out for her, as we spent most of our time in her kitchen, making fudge and eating her special sugar cookies, resulting in waists that no angled elbows could hide.

Grandma was always happy to see us, and told us how pretty we looked—except once. My cousin Maria and I went shopping one afternoon when we were visiting her in Florida. Maria convinced me that I looked incredibly glamorous in a hospital-green linen bomber jacket with puffy sleeves. I was excited about my new and daring look—until Grandma saw it. She had an unmatched ability to cut to the heart of the matter in the nicest possible way. Her reaction to the green fiasco was "That's lovely, dear. But in my day, we tried to buy things that suited us."

Those words echo through my mind whenever I stand in front of a mirror unsure if I am looking at the New Me or just a wildly unflattering experiment. As girls and young women, we all go through many phases, depending on how we feel about ourselves and our bodies. We try to dress like people we admire, the most popular girls in the class, or celebrities of the moment. It takes time to figure out our own conception of beauty—both outer and inner, and often we return to the images of beauty that we formed in our youth, transformed through our lifetime of experience. Thinking about my grandmothers now, I understand that it was their faith, bravery, curiosity, and humor, as well as their fashionable hats, that made them beautiful.

I thought this book should include poems that explore women's complicated relationship with beauty, and our attachments to objects that help us feel and look more attractive. The way we present ourselves to the world, our changing sense of self, the pleasure of feeling pretty, the pain of feeling self-conscious, and the freedom that comes with accepting yourself are all important parts of being a woman.

Shakespeare's description of Cleopatra is one of the most extravagant in all of literature. He makes an explicit connection between beauty and power, describing the elaborate pageantry of Cleopatra's golden barge, her breathtaking loveliness, and the royal authority of her seductive voice. At a time when kings and pharaohs were believed to have divine attributes, and women were powerless and almost nonexistent in the historical record, Cleopatra was truly a wonder of the world.

In contrast, Ralph Waldo Emerson's poem "The Rhodora" contains the observation, "Beauty is its own excuse for being." Writing about a flower hidden in the woods, Emerson ponders the mystery of nature and the existence of effortless beauty. Other poems examine the efforts women go to in order to be beautiful. In "What Do Women Want?" and "Cosmetics Do No Good," the poets describe the irresistible appeal of clothes and makeup.

One of the most surprising poems is "Face Lift" by Sylvia Plath. Written in 1961, well before the explosion of cosmetic surgery, the poem describes the clinical aspects of the procedure. The level of detail is similar to poems in which Plath describes her own shock treatments and hospitalization for mental illness. Interestingly, in the poem she evokes Cleopatra lying naked on her barge, as the patient is wheeled down the hospital corridor into the operating room.

In "The Catch" by Richard Wilbur and "Delight in Disorder" by Robert Herrick, male poets writing three hundred years apart describe the impact of what women wear. Richard Wilbur describes how mystified he feels watching a woman try on a new dress in the mirror. And in "Patterns," Amy Lowell explores the ways in which women rely on clothes to distract us from events we cannot control.

The last word belongs to Marianne Moore, whose complicated poem "Roses Only" ends with the memorable line, "your thorns are the best part of you."

Antony and Cleopatra, II, ii, 191–232

WILLIAM SHAKESPEARE

Enobarbus:

. . . The barge she sat in, like a burnish'd throne
Burn'd on the water: the poop was beaten gold;
Purple the sails, and so perfumed that
The winds were love-sick with them; the oars were silver,
Which to the tune of flutes kept stroke, and made
The water which they beat to follow faster,
As amorous of their strokes. For her own person,
It beggar'd all description: she did lie
In her pavilion—cloth of gold, of tissue—
O'er-picturing that Venus where we see
The fancy outwork nature. On each side her,
Stood pretty dimpled boys, like smiling Cupids,
With divers-colour'd fans, whose wind did seem
To glow the delicate cheeks which they did cool,
And what they undid did.

Agrippa: O, rare for Antony!

Enobarbus:

Her gentlewomen, like the Nereides,
So many mermaids, tended her i' the eyes,
And made their bends adornings. At the helm
A seeming mermaid steers: the silken tackle
Swell with the touches of those flower-soft hands,
That yarely frame the office. From the barge
A strange invisible perfume hits the sense
Of the adjacent wharfs. The city cast
Her people out upon her; and Antony,

Enthron'd i' the market-place, did sit alone,
Whistling to the air; which, but for vacancy,
Had gone to gaze on Cleopatra too,
And made a gap in nature.

Agrippa: Rare Egyptian!

Enobarbus:
Upon her landing, Antony sent to her,
Invited her to supper: she replied,
It should be better he became her guest,
Which she entreated: our courteous Antony,
Whom ne'er the word of 'No' woman heard speak,
Being barber'd ten times o'er, goes to the feast;
And for his ordinary, pays his heart,
For what his eyes eat only.

Agrippa: Royal wench!
She made great Cæsar lay his sword to bed;
He plough'd her, and she cropp'd.

Enobarbus: I saw her once
Hop forty paces through the public street,
And having lost her breath, she spoke, and panted,
That she did make defect perfection,
And, breathless, power breathe forth.

What Do Women Want?

KIM ADDONIZIO

I want a red dress.
I want it flimsy and cheap,
I want it too tight, I want to wear it
until someone tears it off me.
I want it sleeveless and backless,
this dress, so no one has to guess
what's underneath. I want to walk down
the street past Thrifty's and the hardware store
with all those keys glittering in the window,
past Mr. and Mrs. Wong selling day-old
donuts in their café, past the Guerra brothers
slinging pigs from the truck and onto the dolly,
hoisting the slick snouts over their shoulders.
I want to walk like I'm the only
woman on earth and I can have my pick.
I want that red dress bad.
I want it to confirm
your worst fears about me,
to show you how little I care about you
or anything except what
I want. When I find it, I'll pull that garment
from its hanger like I'm choosing a body
to carry me into this world, through
the birth-cries and the love-cries too,
and I'll wear it like bones, like skin,
it'll be the goddamned
dress they bury me in.

The Catch

RICHARD WILBUR

From the dress-box's plashing tis-
Sue paper she pulls out her prize,
Dangling it to one side before my eyes
        Like a weird sort of fish

That she has somehow hooked and gaffed
And on the dock-end holds in air—
Limp, corrugated, lank, a catch too rare
        Not to be photographed.

I, in my chair, make shift to say
Some bright, discerning thing, and fail,
Proving once more the blindness of the male.
        Annoyed, she stalks away

And then is back in half a minute,
Consulting, now, not me at all
But the long mirror, mirror on the wall.
        The dress, now that she's in it,

Has changed appreciably, and gains
By lacy shoes, a light perfume
Whose subtle field electrifies the room,
        And two slim golden chains.

With a fierce frown and hard-pursed lips
She twists a little on her stem
To test the even swirling of the hem,
        Smooths down the waist and hips,

Plucks at the shoulder-straps a bit,
    Then turns around and looks behind,
Her face transfigured now by peace of mind.
    There is no question—it

    Is wholly charming, it is she,
        As I belatedly remark,
And may be hung now in the fragrant dark
        Of her soft armory.

Cosmetics Do No Good

STEVE KOWIT

after Vidyapati

Cosmetics do no good:
no shadow, rouge, mascara, lipstick—
nothing helps.
However artfully I comb my hair,
embellishing my throat & wrists with jewels,
it is no use—there is no
semblance of the beautiful young girl
I was
& long for still.
My loveliness is past.
& no one could be more aware than I am
that coquettishness at this age
only renders me ridiculous.
I know it. Nonetheless,
I primp myself before the glass
like an infatuated schoolgirl
fussing over every detail,
practicing whatever subtlety
may please him.
I cannot help myself.
The God of Passion has his will of me
& I am tossed about
between humiliation & desire,
rectitude & lust,
disintegration & renewal,
ruin & salvation.

Face Lift

SYLVIA PLATH

You bring me good news from the clinic,
Whipping off your silk scarf, exhibiting the tight white
Mummy-cloths, smiling: I'm all right.
When I was nine, a lime-green anesthetist
Fed me banana gas through a frog-mask. The nauseous vault
Boomed with bad dreams and the Jovian voices of surgeons.
Then mother swam up, holding a tin basin.
O I was sick.

They've changed all that. Traveling
Nude as Cleopatra in my well-boiled hospital shift,
Fizzy with sedatives and unusually humorous,
I roll to an anteroom where a kind man
Fists my fingers for me. He makes me feel something precious
Is leaking from the finger-vents. At the count of two
Darkness wipes me out like chalk on a blackboard...
I don't know a thing.

For five days I lie in secret,
Tapped like a cask, the years draining into my pillow.
Even my best friend thinks I'm in the country.
Skin doesn't have roots, it peels away easy as paper.
When I grin, the stitches tauten. I grow backward. I'm twenty,
Broody and in long skirts on my first husband's sofa, my fingers
Buried in the lambswool of the dead poodle;
I hadn't a cat yet.

Now she's done for, the dewlapped lady
I watched settle, line by line, in my mirror—

Old sock-face, sagged on a darning egg.
They've trapped her in some laboratory jar.
Let her die there, or wither incessantly for the next fifty years,
Nodding and rocking and fingering her thin hair.
Mother to myself, I wake swaddled in gauze,
Pink and smooth as a baby.

Fatigue

HILAIRE BELLOC

I'm tired of Love: I'm still more tired of Rhyme.
But Money gives me pleasure all the time.

The Great Lover

RUPERT BROOKE

I have been so great a lover: filled my days
So proudly with the splendor of Love's praise,
The pain, the calm, and the astonishment,
Desire illimitable, and still content,
And all dear names men use, to cheat despair,
For the perplexed and viewless streams that bear
Our hearts at random down the dark of life.
Now, ere the unthinking silence on that strife
Steals down, I would cheat drowsy Death so far,
My night shall be remembered for a star
That outshone all the suns of all men's days.
Shall I not crown them with immortal praise
Whom I have loved, who have given me, dared with me
High secrets, and in darkness knelt to see
The inenarrable godhead of delight?
Love is a flame:—we have beaconed the world's night.
A city:—and we have built it, these and I.
An emperor:—we have taught the world to die.
So, for their sakes I loved, ere I go hence,
And the high cause of Love's magnificence.
And to keep loyalties young, I'll write those names
Golden for ever, eagles, crying flames,
And set them as a banner, that men may know,
To dare the generations, burn, and blow
Out on the wind of Time, shining and streaming. . . .

These I have loved:
        White plates and cups, clean-gleaming,
Ringed with blue lines; and feathery, faëry dust;

Wet roofs, beneath the lamp-light; the strong crust
Of friendly bread; and many-tasting food;
Rainbows; and the blue bitter smoke of wood;
And radiant raindrops couching in cool flowers;
And flowers themselves, that sway through sunny hours,
Dreaming of moths that drink them under the moon;
Then, the cool kindliness of sheets, that soon
Smooth away trouble; and the rough male kiss
Of blankets; grainy wood; live hair that is
Shining and free; blue-massing clouds; the keen
Unpassioned beauty of a great machine;
The benison of hot water; furs to touch;
The good smell of old clothes; and other such—
The comfortable smell of friendly fingers,
Hair's fragrance, and the musty reek that lingers
About dead leaves and last year's ferns....

                              Dear names,
And thousand others throng to me! Royal flames;
Sweet water's dimpling laugh from tap or spring;
Holes in the ground; and voices that do sing:
Voices in laughter, too; and body's pain,
Soon turned to peace: and the deep-panting train;
Firm sands; the little dulling edge of foam
That browns and dwindles as the wave goes home;
And washen stones, gay for an hour; the cold
Graveness of iron; moist black earthen mold;
Sleep; and high places; footprints in the dew;
And oaks; and brown horse-chestnuts, glossy-new;
And new-peeled sticks; and shining pools on grass;—
All these have been my loves. And these shall pass,
Whatever passes not, in the great hour,
Nor all my passion, all my prayers, have power
To hold them with me through the gate of Death.

They'll play deserter, turn with the traitor breath,
Break the high bond we made, and sell Love's trust
And sacramental covenant to the dust.
—Oh, never a doubt but, somewhere, I shall wake,
And give what's left of love again, and make
New friends now strangers....

                              But the best I've known
Stays here, and changes, breaks, grows old, is blown
About the winds of the world, and fades from brains
Of living men, and dies.

                    Nothing remains.

O dear my loves, O faithless, once again
This one last gift I give: that after men
Shall know, and later lovers, far-removed
Praise you, "All these were lovely"; say, "He loved."

Patterns

AMY LOWELL

I walk down the garden paths,
And all the daffodils
Are blowing, and the bright blue squills.
I walk down the patterned garden-paths
In my stiff, brocaded gown.
With my powdered hair and jeweled fan,
I too am a rare
Pattern. As I wander down
The garden paths.

My dress is richly figured,
And the train
Makes a pink and silver stain
On the gravel, and the thrift
Of the borders.
Just a plate of current fashion,
Tripping by in high-heeled, ribboned shoes.
Not a softness anywhere about me,
Only whalebone and brocade.
And I sink on a seat in the shade
Of a lime tree. For my passion
Wars against the stiff brocade.
The daffodils and squills
Flutter in the breeze
As they please.
And I weep;
For the lime-tree is in blossom
And one small flower has dropped upon my bosom.

And the plashing of waterdrops
In the marble fountain
Comes down the garden-paths.
The dripping never stops.
Underneath my stiffened gown
Is the softness of a woman bathing in a marble basin,
A basin in the midst of hedges grown
So thick, she cannot see her lover hiding,
But she guesses he is near,
And the sliding of the water
Seems the stroking of a dear
Hand upon her.
What is Summer in a fine brocaded gown!
I should like to see it lying in a heap upon the ground.
All the pink and silver crumpled up on the ground.

I would be the pink and silver as I ran along the paths,
And he would stumble after,
Bewildered by my laughter.
I should see the sun flashing from his sword-hilt and the buckles
    on his shoes.
I would choose
To lead him in a maze along the patterned paths,
A bright and laughing maze for my heavy-booted lover.
Till he caught me in the shade,
And the buttons of his waistcoat bruised my body as he
    clasped me,
Aching, melting, unafraid.
With the shadows of the leaves and the sundrops,
And the plopping of the waterdrops,
All about us in the open afternoon—
I am very like to swoon

With the weight of this brocade,
For the sun sifts through the shade.

Underneath the fallen blossom
In my bosom,
Is a letter I have hid.
It was brought to me this morning by a rider from the Duke.
"Madam, we regret to inform you that Lord Hartwell
Died in action Thursday se'nnight."
As I read it in the white, morning sunlight,
The letters squirmed like snakes.
"Any answer, Madam," said my footman.
"No," I told him.
"See that the messenger takes some refreshment.
No, no answer."
And I walked into the garden,
Up and down the patterned paths,
In my stiff, correct brocade.
The blue and yellow flowers stood up proudly in the sun,
Each one.
I stood upright too,
Held rigid to the pattern
By the stiffness of my gown.
Up and down I walked,
Up and down.

In a month he would have been my husband.
In a month, here, underneath this lime,
We would have broke the pattern;
He for me, and I for him,
He as Colonel, I as Lady,
On this shady seat.
He had a whim

That sunlight carried blessing.
And I answered, "It shall be as you have said."
Now he is dead.

In Summer and in Winter I shall walk
Up and down
The patterned garden-paths
In my stiff, brocaded gown.
The squills and daffodils
Will give place to pillared roses, and to asters, and to snow.
I shall go
Up and down,
In my gown.
Gorgeously arrayed,
Boned and stayed.
And the softness of my body will be guarded from embrace
By each button, hook, and lace.
For the man who should loose me is dead,
Fighting with the Duke in Flanders,
In a pattern called a war.
Christ! What are patterns for?

Crocheted Bag

ROSEMARY CATACALOS

Habibi, I want to *live* the string bag from Bahrain—a birthday
     you say—
with its brazen blue mouth and deep yellow light always rising
     from
below. Clearly a woman's work, stitches through which the air
     shines,
and the things within are apparent from without. A woman's days
laced together, only closed enough to contain her faith. A woman's
fishing net, her dream, which, if slept upon, would mark the skin
with equal-armed crosses that say the center is everywhere.
     As grape
leaves the world over are seasoned with the same sun. As no child
anywhere should ever want to die. A woman's prayer, with
     handles
top *and* bottom so always the load can be slung between two
walkers on the same path.

Delight in Disorder

ROBERT HERRICK

A sweet disorder in the dress
Kindles in clothes a wantonness:
A lawn about the shoulders thrown
Into a fine distraction:
An erring lace, which here and there
Enthrals the crimson stomacher:
A cuff neglectful, and thereby
Ribbons to flow confusedly:
A winning wave, deserving note,
In the tempestuous petticoat:
A careless shoe-string, in whose tie
I see a wild civility:
Do more bewitch me than when art
Is too precise in every part.

The Rhodora

On Being Asked, Whence Is the Flower?

RALPH WALDO EMERSON

In May, when sea-winds pierced our solitudes,
I found the fresh Rhodora in the woods,
Spreading its leafless blooms in a damp nook,
To please the desert and the sluggish brook.
The purple petals, fallen in the pool,
Made the black water with their beauty gay;
Here might the red-bird come his plumes to cool,
And court the flower that cheapens his array.
Rhodora! if the sages ask thee why
This charm is wasted on the earth and sky,
Tell them, dear, that if eyes were made for seeing,
Then Beauty is its own excuse for being:
Why thou wert there, O rival of the rose!
I never thought to ask, I never knew:
But, in my simple ignorance, suppose
The self-same Power that brought me there brought you.

Roses Only

MARIANNE MOORE

You do not seem to realize that beauty is a liability rather than
    an asset—that in view of the fact that spirit creates form we are
        justified in supposing
            that you must have brains. For you, a symbol of the unit, stiff
                and sharp,
        conscious of surpassing by dint of native superiority and liking
            for everything
self-dependent, anything an

ambitious civilization might produce: for you, unaided, to attempt
        through sheer
    reserve to confute presumptions resulting from observation is
        idle. You cannot make us
            think you a delightful happen-so. But rose, if you are brilliant,
                it
        is not because your petals are the without-which-nothing of pre-
            eminence. You would look, minus
thorns—like a what-is-this, a mere

peculiarity. They are not proof against a storm, the elements, or
        mildew
    but what about the predatory hand? What is brilliance without
        coordination? Guarding the
            infinitesimal pieces of your mind, compelling audience to
        the remark that it is better to be forgotten than to be
            remembered too violently,
your thorns are the best part of you.

Eagle Poem

JOY HARJO

To pray you open your whole self
To sky, to earth, to sun, to moon
To one whole voice that is you.
And know there is more
That you can't see, can't hear;
Can't know except in moments
Steadly growing, and in languages
That aren't always sound but other
Circles of motion.
Like eagle that Sunday morning
Over Salt River. Circled in blue sky
In wind, swept our hearts clean
With sacred wings.
We see you, see ourselves and know
That we must take the utmost care
And kindness in all things.
Breathe in, knowing we are made of
All this, and breathe, knowing
We are truly blessed because we
Were born, and die soon within a
True circle of motion,
Like eagle rounding out the morning
Inside us.
We pray that it will be done
In beauty.
In beauty.

MOTHERHOOD

*M*Y CHILDREN ARE too wonderful and too old for me to write about them without getting into trouble. But I can certainly say, like everyone does, that becoming a mother is the best thing that ever happened to me. Having a child defines us for the rest of our lives. No matter what else we do, we will always be that person's mother. We give our children the gift of ourselves, and they give us so much more in return—especially when they are teenagers! Each mother-child relationship teaches us our limitations and our strengths. It changes us in constantly unfolding ways and entwines us in the unpredictable mystery of another life.

The poems in this section start and end with a blessing. They begin with "A Cradle Song" by W. B. Yeats, a lullaby of wonder from a parent to a newborn child. The last poem is Lucille Clifton's "blessing the boats," in which she wishes safe passage for a child whose mother's arms can no longer protect her from the world.

In motherhood, like poetry, the particular becomes universal. Each detail evokes an entire world of memories. In "Socks," Sharon Olds describes the feeling of being needed as she lifts her lazy son's leg to put on his sock, and every mother can feel the dead weight of that heavy leg with her own muscle memory.

There are also poems about mothers from the child's point of view. In "Clearances," the special closeness Seamus Heaney felt when he and his mother peeled potatoes together reminds us that sharing the mundane duties of daily life builds a lifetime of love between parent and child.

The old-fashioned poem "Somebody's Mother" by Mary Dow Brine, shares an important theme with Elizabeth Alexander's modern works "The Dream That I Told My Mother-in-Law" and "Ode." One of the great gifts of motherhood is the ability to see other people's children as our own, and to feel that the responsibility of caring for them is ours.

My aunt Eunice, who founded the Special Olympics, used to quote Henry Ward Beecher, who wrote, "A mother's heart is a child's schoolroom." Our mothers are our first teachers, and we teach others the same lessons we learn from them. As a child, when your mother believes in you, you believe in yourself, and when that happens, there is nothing you can't do. As a mother, that is the greatest gift we can give to a child.

A Cradle Song

W. B. YEATS

The angels are stooping
Above your bed;
They weary of trooping
With the whimpering dead.

God's laughing in Heaven
To see you so good;
The Sailing Seven
Are gay with His mood.

I sigh that kiss you,
For I must own
That I shall miss you
When you have grown.

Notes from the Delivery Room

LINDA PASTAN

Strapped down,
victim in an old comic book,
I have been here before,
this place where pain winces
off the walls
like too bright light.
Bear down a doctor says,
foreman to sweating laborer,
but this work, this forcing
of one life from another
is something that I signed for
at a moment when I would have signed anything.
Babies should grow in fields;
common as beets or turnips
they should be picked and held
root end up, soil spilling
from between their toes—
and how much easier it would be later,
returning them to earth.
Bear up ... bear down ... the audience
grows restive, and I'm a new magician
who can't produce the rabbit
from my swollen hat.
She's crowning, someone says,
but there is no one royal here,
just me, quite barefoot,
greeting my barefoot child.

Socks

SHARON OLDS

I'll play Ninja Death with you
tonight, if you buy new socks, I say
to our son. After supper he holds out his foot,
the sock with a hole for its heel, I whisk it
into the wastebasket. He is tired, allergic,
his hands full of Ninja Death leaflets,
I take a sock from the bag, heft his
Achilles tendon in my palm and pull the
cotton over the arch and instep,
I have not done this for years, I feel
intensely happy, drawing the sock
up the calf—*Other foot*—
as if we are back in the days of my great
usefulness. We cast the dice
for how we will fight, I *swing* my *mace,*
he *ducks, parries* with his *chain,* I'm *dazed,* then
stunned. Day after day, year after
year I dressed our little beloveds
as if it were a life's work,
stretching the necks of the shirts to get them
over their heads, guarding the nape as I
swooped them on their back to slide overalls on—
back through the toddler clothes to the one-year
clothes to those gauzy infant-suits that un-
snapped along each seam to lie
fully open, like the body first offered to the
soul to clothe it, the mother given to the child.

High School Senior

SHARON OLDS

For seventeen years, her breath in the house
at night, puff, puff, like summer
cumulus above her bed,
and her scalp smelling of apricots
—this being who had formed within me,
squatted like a bright tree-frog in the dark,
like an eohippus she had come out of history
slowly, through me, into the daylight,
I had the daily sight of her,
like food or air she was there, like a mother.
I say "college," but I feel as if I cannot tell
the difference between her leaving for college
and our parting forever—I try to see
this house without her, without her pure
depth of feeling, without her creek-brown
hair, her daedal hands with their tapered
fingers, her pupils dark as the mourning cloak's
wing, but I can't. Seventeen years
ago, in this room, she moved inside me,
I looked at the river, I could not imagine
my life with her. I gazed across the street,
and saw, in the icy winter sun,
a column of steam rush up away from the earth.
There are creatures whose children float away
at birth, and those who throat-feed their young
for weeks and never see them again. My daughter
is free and she is in me—no, my love
of her is in me, moving in my heart,
changing chambers, like something poured
from hand to hand, to be weighed and then reweighed.

Nobody Knows But Mother

MARY MORRISON

How many buttons are missing today?
   Nobody knows but Mother.
How many playthings are strewn in her way?
   Nobody knows but Mother.
How many thimbles and spools has she missed?
How many burns on each fat little fist?
How many bumps to be cuddled and kissed?
   Nobody knows but Mother.

How many hats has she hunted today?
   Nobody knows but Mother.
Carelessly hiding themselves in the hay—
   Nobody knows but Mother.
How many handkerchiefs wilfully strayed?
How many ribbons for each little maid?
How for her care can a mother be paid?
   Nobody knows but Mother.

How many muddy shoes all in a row?
   Nobody knows but Mother.
How many stockings to darn, do you know?
   Nobody knows but Mother.
How many little torn aprons to mend?
How many hours of toil must she spend?
What is the time when her day's work shall end?
   Nobody knows but Mother.

How many lunches for Tommy and Sam?
   Nobody knows but Mother.

Cookies and apples and blackberry jam—
    Nobody knows but Mother.
Nourishing dainties for every "sweet tooth,"
Toddling Dottie or dignified Ruth—
How much love sweetens the labor, forsooth?
    Nobody knows but Mother.

How many cares does a mother's heart know?
    Nobody knows but Mother.
How many joys from her mother love flow?
    Nobody knows but Mother.
How many prayers for each little white bed?
How many tears for her babes has she shed?
How many kisses for each curly head?
    Nobody knows but Mother.

From *"Clearances," In Memoriam M.K.H. (1911–1984)*

SEAMUS HEANEY

When all the others were away at Mass
I was all hers as we peeled potatoes.
They broke the silence, let fall one by one
Like solder weeping off the soldering iron:
Cold comforts set between us, things to share
Gleaming in a bucket of clean water.
And again let fall. Little pleasant splashes
From each other's work would bring us to our senses.

So while the parish priest at her bedside
Went hammer and tongs at the prayers for the dying
And some were responding and some crying
I remembered her head bent towards my head,
Her breath in mine, our fluent dipping knives—
Never closer the whole rest of our lives.

Woman's Work

JULIA ALVAREZ

for Judy Yarnall

Who says a woman's work isn't high art?
She challenged as she scrubbed the bathroom tiles.
Keep house as if the address were your heart.

We cleaned the whole upstairs before we started
downstairs. I sighed, hearing my friends outside.
Doing her woman's work was a hard art

to practice when the summer sun would bar
the floor I swept till she was satisfied.
She kept me prisoner in her housebound heart.

She shined the tines of forks, the wheels of carts,
cut lacy lattices for all her pies.
Her woman's work was nothing less than art.

And I, her masterpiece since I was smart,
was primed, praised, polished, scolded, and advised
to keep a house much better than my heart.

I did not want to be her counterpart!
I struck out . . . but became my mother's child:
a woman working at home on her art,
housekeeping paper as if it were her heart.

if there are any heavens my mother will(all by herself)have

E. E. CUMMINGS

if there are any heavens my mother will(all by herself)have
one. It will not be a pansy heaven nor
a fragile heaven of lilies-of-the-valley but
it will be a heaven of blackred roses

my father will be (deep like a rose
tall like a rose)

standing near my

(swaying over her
silent)
with eyes which are really petals and see

nothing with the face of a poet really which
is a flower and not a face with
hands
which whisper
This is my beloved my

                        (suddenly in sunlight
he will bow,

& the whole garden will bow)

Somebody's Mother

MARY DOW BRINE

The woman was old and ragged and gray
And bent with the chill of the Winter's day.

The street was wet with a recent snow
And the woman's feet were aged and slow.

She stood at the crossing and waited long,
Alone, uncared for, amid the throng

Of human beings who passed her by
Nor heeded the glance of her anxious eye.

Down the street, with laughter and shout,
Glad in the freedom of "school let out,"

Came the boys like a flock of sheep,
Hailing the snow piled white and deep.

Past the woman so old and gray
Hastened the children on their way.

Nor offered a helping hand to her—
So meek, so timid, afraid to stir

Lest the carriage wheels or the horses' feet
Should crowd her down in the slippery street.

At last came one of the merry troop,
The gayest laddie of all the group;

He paused beside her and whispered low,
"I'll help you cross, if you wish to go."

Her aged hand on his strong young arm
She placed, and so, without hurt or harm,

He guided the trembling feet along,
Proud that his own were firm and strong.

Then back again to his friends he went,
His young heart happy and well content.

"She's somebody's mother, boys, you know,
For all she's aged and poor and slow,

"And I hope some fellow will lend a hand
To help my mother, you understand,

"If ever she's poor and old and gray,
When her own dear boy is far away."

And "somebody's mother" bowed low her head
In her home that night, and the prayer she said

Was, "God be kind to the noble boy,
Who is somebody's son, and pride and joy!"

And Ruth said,
Intreat me not to leave thee,
or to return from following after thee:
For whither thou goest,
I will go;
and where thou lodgest,
I will lodge.
Thy people shall be my people,
and thy God my God.

Where thou diest, will I die,
and there will I be buried.
The Lord do so to me, and more also,
if aught but death part thee and me.

The Dream That I Told My Mother-in-Law

ELIZABETH ALEXANDER

In the room almost filled with our bed,
the small bedroom, the king-sized bed high up
and on casters so sometimes we would roll,
in the room in the corner of the corner
apartment on top of a hill so the bed would roll,
we felt as if we might break off and drift,
float, and become our own continent.
When your mother first entered our apartment
she went straight to that room and libated our bed
with water from your homeland. Soon she saw
in my cheeks the fire and poppy stain,
and soon thereafter on that bed came the boy.
Then months, then the morning I cracked first one
then two then three eggs in a white bowl
and all had double yolks, and your mother
(now our mother) read the signs. Signs everywhere,
signs rampant, a season of signs and a vial
of white dirt brought across three continents
to the enormous white bed that rolled
and now held three, and soon held four,
four on the bed, two boys, one man, and me,
our mother reading all signs and blessing our bed,
blessing our bed filled with babies, blessing our bed
through her frailty, blessing us and our bed,
blessing us and our bed.

                      She began to dream
of childhood flowers, her long-gone parents.
I told her my dream in a waiting room:

a photographer photographed women,
said her portraits revealed their truest selves.
She snapped my picture, peeled back the paper,
and there was my son's face, my first son, my self.
Mamma loved that dream so I told it again.
And soon she crossed over to her parents,
sisters, one son (War took that son.
We destroy one another), and women came
by twos and tens wrapped in her same fine white
bearing huge pans of stew, round breads, homemade wines,
and men came in suits with their ravaged faces
and together they cried and cried and cried
and keened and cried and the sound
was a live hive swelling and growing,
all the water in the world, all the salt, all the wails,
and the sound grew too big for the building and finally
lifted what needed to be lifted from the casket and we quieted
and watched it waft up and away like feather, like ash.
Daughter, she said, when her journey began, *You are a mother now,*
and you have to take care of the world.

Mother's Closet

MAXINE SCATES

This is everything she ever closed a door
on, the broom closet of childhood
where no one could ever find a broom.
Here, layer upon layer, nothing breathes:
photo albums curl at the edges, books
she brought home from the library
where she worked, handled by thousands
of other hands before their final exile
where they've waited, paper and more paper
taking in the ocean air, about to sprout.

Mother's sitting on the bed
with her tattered list of dispersals—who gets
what among the treasures she hopes
I'll find, but I know I'm seeing
what she doesn't want me to see,
the daughter cleaning doing what the son
would never do. After an hour of excavation
the console TV emerges from beneath
forgotten sweaters and balled up nylons
saved for stuffing puppets, a long ago church project—
the TV arrived in 1966 same day I crushed
the fender of the car, upsetting
the careful plans she'd made for payment.

She wants to leave so much behind. Hours later
I've found nothing I want but the purple mache mask
I made in the fourth grade. I like its yellow eyes.
She looks at each magazine I remove, saving

every word about my brother, the coach. He's sixty
and a long dead mouse has eaten the laces
of his baby shoes. I want order. I say
I'm old myself, I've started throwing things away.
I'm lying. I've kept everything she's ever given me.

Ode

ELIZABETH ALEXANDER

I love all the mom bodies at this beach,
the tummies, the one-piece bathing suits,
the bosoms that slope, the wide nice bottoms,
thigh flesh shirred as gentle wind shirrs a pond.

So many sensible haircuts and ponytails!
These bodies show they have grown babies, then
nourished them, woken to their cries, fretted
at their fevers. Biceps have lifted and toted

the babies now printed on their mothers.
"If you lined up a hundred vaginas,
I could tell you which ones have borne children,"
the midwife says. In the secret place or

in sunlight at the beach, our bodies say
This is who we are, no, This is what
we have done and continue to do.
We labor in love. We do it. We mother.

Vietnam

WISLAWA SZYMBORSKA

"Woman, what's your name?" "I don't know."
"How old are you? Where are you from?" "I don't know."
"Why did you dig that burrow?" "I don't know."
"How long have you been hiding?" "I don't know."
"Why did you bite my finger?" "I don't know."
"Don't you know that we won't hurt you?" "I don't know."
"Whose side are you on?" "I don't know."
"This is war, you've got to choose." "I don't know."
"Does your village still exist?" "I don't know."
"Are those your children?" "Yes."

A Child

MARY LAMB

A child's a plaything for an hour;
    Its pretty tricks we try
For that or for a longer space—
    Then tire, and lay it by.

But I knew one that to itself
    All seasons could control;
That would have mock'd the sense of pain
    Out of a grievéd soul.

Thou straggler into loving arms,
    Young climber-up of knees,
When I forget thy thousand ways
    Then life and all shall cease.

blessing the boats

LUCILLE CLIFTON

(at St. Mary's)

may the tide
that is entering even now
the lip of our understanding
carry you out
beyond the face of fear
may you kiss
the wind then turn from it
certain that it will
love your back   may you
open your eyes to water
water waving forever
and may you in your innocence
sail through this to that

SILENCE AND SOLITUDE

*W*E ARE ALL AFRAID of being alone. To teenagers, the idea of being alone is almost as bad as the idea of dying, which at least has a certain romantic appeal. But by the time women have young children, we would sacrifice almost anything to be by ourselves in a quiet house—if just for an hour. As we reach middle age, the fear returns. Every woman I know is filled with dread at the prospect of an empty nest. Though our sons may tower over us, and our daughters know more than we do about everything, we still wait up to make sure they are safely home, we volunteer to drive them miles out of our way hoping for a few moments of conversation, we clean their filthy rooms, and offer to give them things they don't particularly want. Just when our children are about to go out in the world as we raised them to, we realize we have become as dependent on them as they are on us.

Middle age is a time to rearrange our lives and enjoy the chance to reflect rather than react. Silence and solitude may take some getting used to, but in my experience, the people who are happy being alone are often the people everyone wants to be around.

Involuntary solitude is another story. The pain of loss, the terror of being abandoned, or an echoing loneliness forces us to confront the most fundamental questions of existence and mortality.

Perseverance, fortitude, and faith can help us salvage meaning and connection out of emotional devastation. Reading and writing poetry can help us find a pathway. Poets put universal feelings into words and remind us that in a world of language and feeling, we can never really be alone.

Often, poets celebrate the freedom of solitude. Emily Brontë and Rainer Maria Rilke write of the exhilaration of being unfettered by the world. Li Po, the eighth-century Chinese poet, writes of surrendering to nature and merging with something larger than oneself. Each of these strategies can help us accept the times in our lives when we may be alone, to appreciate them, and to learn from them.

One of my favorite lines of poetry is found in Wallace Stevens's "The Poems of Our Climate." Stevens describes a world from which everything has been subtracted, leaving only stillness and a bowl of white carnations. Yet the room is full, because of the presence of the "never resting mind." Through our humanity, we have the power to create new worlds, alone and with others. Stevens concludes with a line celebrating life: "The imperfect is our paradise." A feeling that women can surely embrace.

I'm happiest when most away

EMILY BRONTË

I'm happiest when most away
I can bear my soul from its home of clay
On a windy night when the moon is bright
And my eye can wander through worlds of light

When I am not and none beside
Nor earth nor sea nor cloudless sky
But only spirit wandering wide
Through infinite immensity

Keeping Things Whole

MARK STRAND

In a field
I am the absence
of field.
This is
always the case.
Wherever I am
I am what is missing.

When I walk
I part the air
and always
the air moves in
to fill the spaces
where my body's been.

We all have reasons
for moving.
I move
to keep things whole.

We All Know It

MARIANNE MOORE

That silence is best: that action and re-
Action are equal: that control, discipline, and
Liberation are bywords when spoken by an appraiser, that the
   Accidental sometimes achieves perfection, loath though
      we may be to admit it:

And that the realm of art is the realm in
Which to look for "fishbones in the throat of the gang." Pin-
Pricks and the unstereotyped embarrassment being the contin-
   Ual diet of artists. And in spite of it all, poets ask us just what it

Is in them that we cannot subscribe to:
People overbear till told to stop: no matter through
What sobering process they have gone, some inquire if emotion,
   true
      And stimulated are not the same thing: promoters request us to
         take our oath

That appearances are not cosmic: mis-
Fits in the world of achievement want to know what bus-
Iness people have to reserve judgment about undertakings. It is
   A strange idea that one must say what one thinks in order to
      be understood.

As Much As You Can

CONSTANTINE P. CAVAFY

And if you can't shape your life the way you want,
at least try as much as you can
not to degrade it
by too much contact with the world,
by too much activity and talk.

Try not to degrade it by dragging it along,
taking it around and exposing it so often
to the daily silliness
of social events and parties,
until it comes to seem a boring hanger-on.

The Heart of a Woman

GEORGIA DOUGLAS JOHNSON

The heart of a woman goes forth with the dawn
As a lone bird, soft winging, so restlessly on;
Afar o'er life's turrets and vales does it roam
In the wake of those echoes the heart calls home.

The heart of a woman falls back with the night,
And enters some alien cage in its plight,
And tries to forget it has dreamed of the stars
While it breaks, breaks, breaks on the sheltering bars.

Sense of Something Coming

RAINER MARIA RILKE

I am like a flag in the center of open space.
I sense ahead the wind which is coming, and must live it through,
While the creatures of the world beneath still do not move
   in their sleep:
The doors still close softly, and the chimneys are full of silence,
The windows do not rattle yet, and the dust still lies down.

I already know the storm, and I am as troubled as the sea,
And spread myself out, and fall into myself,
And throw myself out and am absolutely alone
In the great storm.

Death, Etc.

MAXINE KUMIN

I have lived my whole life with death, said William Maxwell,
aetat ninety-one, and haven't we all. Amen to that.
It's all right to gutter out like a candle but the odds are better

for succumbing to a stroke or pancreatic cancer.
I'm not being gloomy, this bright September
when everything around me shines with being:

hummingbirds still raptured in the jewelweed,
puffballs humping up out of the forest duff
and the whole voluptuous garden still putting forth

bright yellow pole beans, deep-pleated purple cauliflowers,
to say nothing of regal white corn that feeds us
night after gluttonous night, with a slobber of butter.

Still, Maxwell's pronouncement speaks to my body's core,
this old body I trouble to keep up the way
I keep up my two old horses, wiping insect deterrent

on their ears, cleaning the corners of their eyes,
spraying their legs to defeat the gnats, currying burrs
out of their thickening coats. They go on grazing thoughtlessly

while winter is gathering in the wings. But it is not given
to us to travel blindly, all the pasture bars down,
to seek out the juiciest grasses, nor to predict

which of these two will predecease the other or to anticipate
the desperate whinnies for the missing that will ensue.
Which of us will go down first is also not given,

a subject that hangs unspoken between us
as with Jocasta, who begs Oedipus not to inquire further.
Meanwhile, it is pleasant to share opinions and mealtimes,

to swim together daily, I with my long slow back and forths,
he with his hundred freestyle strokes that wind him alarmingly.
A sinker, he would drown if he did not flail like this.

We have put behind us the State Department tour
of Egypt, Israel, Thailand, Japan that ended badly
as we leapt down the yellow chutes to safety after a botched takeoff.

We have been made at home in Belgium, Holland, and Switzerland,
narrow, xenophobic Switzerland of clean bathrooms and much butter.
We have traveled by Tube and Métro *in the realms of gold*

paid obeisance to the Winged Victory and the dreaded Tower,
but now it is time to settle as the earth itself settles
in season, exhaling, dozing a little before the fall rains come.

Every August when the family gathers, we pose
under the ancient willow for a series of snapshots,
the same willow, its lumpish trunk sheathed in winking aluminum

that so perplexed us forty years ago, before we understood
the voracity of porcupines. Now hollowed by age and marauders,
its aluminum girdle painted dull brown, it is still leafing

out at the top, still housing a tumult of goldfinches. We try to
   hold still
and smile, squinting into the brilliance, the middle-aged children,
the grown grandsons, the dogs of each era, always a pair

of grinning shelter dogs whose long lives are but as grasshoppers
compared to our own. We try to live gracefully
and at peace with our imagined deaths but in truth we go forward

stumbling, afraid of the dark,
of the cold, and of the great overwhelming
loneliness of being last.

GALWAY KINNELL

7

When one has lived a long time alone,
one likes alike the pig, who brooks no deferment
of gratification, and the porcupine, or thorned pig,
who enters the cellar but not the house itself
because of eating down the cellar stairs on the way up,
and one likes the worm, who by bunching herself together
and expanding works her way through the ground,
no less than the butterfly, who totters full of worry
among the day lilies, as they darken,
and more and more one finds one likes
any other species better than one's own,
which has gone amok, making one self-estranged,
when one has lived a long time alone.

9

When one has lived a long time alone,
and the hermit thrush calls and there is an answer,
and the bullfrog head half out of water utters
the cantillations he sang in his first spring,
and the snake lowers himself over the threshold
and creeps away among the stones, one sees
they all live to mate with their kind, and one knows,
after a long time of solitude, after the many steps taken
away from one's kind, toward these other kingdoms,
the hard prayer inside one's own singing
is to come back, if one can, to one's own,
a world almost lost, in the exile that deepens,
when one has lived a long time alone.

10

When one has lived a long time alone,
one wants to live again among men and women,
to return to that place where one's ties with the human
broke, where the disquiet of death and now also
of history glimmers its firelight on faces,
where the gaze of the new baby meets the gaze
of the great granny, and where lovers speak,
on lips blowsy from kissing, that language
the same in each mouth, and like birds at daybreak
blether the song that is both earth's and heaven's,
until the sun rises, and they stand
in the daylight of being made one: kingdom come,
when one has lived a long time alone.

Zazen on Ching-t'ing Mountain

LI PO

The birds have vanished down the sky,
Now the last cloud drains away.

We sit together, the mountain and me,
until only the mountain remains.

The Poems of Our Climate

WALLACE STEVENS

I

Clear water in a brilliant bowl,
Pink and white carnations. The light
In the room more like a snowy air,
Reflecting snow. A newly-fallen snow
At the end of winter when afternoons return.
Pink and white carnations–one desires
So much more than that. The day itself
Is simplified: a bowl of white,
Cold, a cold porcelain, low and round,
With nothing more than the carnations here.

II

Say even that this complete simplicity
Stripped one of all one's torments, concealed
The evilly compounded, vital I
And made it fresh in a world of white,
A world of clear water, brilliant-edged,
Still one would want more, one would need more,
More than a world of white and snowy scents.

III

There would still remain the never-resting mind,
So that one would want to escape, come back
To what had been so long composed.
The imperfect is our paradise.
Note that, in this bitterness, delight,
Since the imperfect is so hot in us,
Lies in flawed words and stubborn sounds.

GROWING UP AND
GROWING OLD

*T*HIS BOOK BEGAN as a collection of poems for middle-aged women—something no one wants to be. When I turned fifty, it seemed that looking old was the only topic of conversation, everyone was bursting into tears at a moment's notice, and proclaiming the importance of taking "time for yourself." On a more serious level, midlife can be a time of reflection and self-reflection, when some of the chaos of raising a family subsides, we have become aware that time is precious, and we have learned what matters. Poems speak directly to those emotions.

Middle age is a time of transition. If we have raised a family, they are beginning to be independent. If we are going back to work, our skills may be outdated. If we have a career, we may be facing the limits of our advancement. If we are caring for our parents, it is becoming a more complicated undertaking. But we are also still young, we have the chance for a full life ahead, and we know ourselves much better than we did.

In order to plan the future, it helps to look back at the decisions we have made so far—even the bad ones. We are reminded of other times when life seemed confusing, emotions overwhelming,

and the pathway forward hard to find. In this section, I have combined poems that speak to us at midlife with those that address another time of transition—growing up and becoming an adult. At both points in our lives, we are faced with a lot of uncertainty and the realization that, although we share these challenges with our friends, we must navigate them on our own. That can be both liberating and terrifying.

The choices we make during these transitions determine who we are and who we become. Poems can help us find clarity amid the confusion. They remind us that others have faced the same challenges. They celebrate the relationships that define and guide us, they can help us laugh at ourselves, and they provide wisdom and reassurance.

Each stage of life is different than we imagine it will be. Edna St. Vincent Millay captures this feeling perfectly in "Grown-up" when she is confronted with the routine of adult life, after fantasizing it to be so much more glamorous. Ellen Hagan captures the contradictory feelings of growing up fast and too fast in "Puberty—With Capital Letters," while Parneshia Jones brings to life the conflicts between mother and daughter that repeat from generation to generation, despite our vows to be different.

In "Older, Younger, Both," Joyce Sutphen conveys the mixed-up sensations of being young and old all at once, a feeling which is common to our teenage years and one that characterizes middle age. Other poems, like Barbara Ras's "You Can't Have It All" and Elizabeth Jennings's "Old Woman," celebrate the contentment that comes with appreciating what we have.

Each of these poets can offer guidance, provide insight, and give us strength. But in these turbulent times each of us must answer the question posed by Mary Oliver in "The Summer Day": "Tell me, what is it you plan to do/with your one wild and precious life?"

You Begin

MARGARET ATWOOD

You begin this way:
this is your hand,
this is your eye,
that is a fish, blue and flat
on the paper, almost
the shape of an eye.
This is your mouth, this is an O
or a moon, whichever
you like. This is yellow.

Outside the window
is the rain, green
because it is summer, and beyond that
the trees and then the world,
which is round and has only
the colors of these nine crayons.

This is the world, which is fuller
and more difficult to learn than I have said.
You are right to smudge it that way
with the red and then
the orange: the world burns.

Once you have learned these words
you will learn that there are more
words than you can ever learn.
The word *hand* floats above your hand
like a small cloud over a lake.

The word *hand* anchors
your hand to this table,
your hand is a warm stone
I hold between two words.

This is your hand, these are my hands, this is the world,
which is round but not flat and has more colors
than we can see.
It begins, it has an end,
this is what you will
come back to, this is your hand.

Grown-up

EDNA ST. VINCENT MILLAY

Was it for this I uttered prayers,
And sobbed and cursed and kicked the stairs,
That now, domestic as a plate,
I should retire at half-past eight?

Puberty—With Capital Letters

ELLEN HAGAN

There went being a kid. There went
Barbie dolls, baby dolls, kitchen sets, play-
doh, crayons, make-believe (well, maybe not
make-believe). But there went innocent, child-
like, there went one-piece bathing suits. In came
adolescence, even though I'd had my period
since I was 10. In came self-consciousness,
waiting for breasts. In came attitude, and "Why
can't I?" "You said!" "I hate you," under my breath.
In came diaries with hidden messages and dares
I always took. In came kissing and not kissing,
and doing it, and not doing it, and rounding bases,
and not rounding bases, and rounding bases having
nothing at all to do with baseball, and sometimes wishing
you could just play baseball instead.

In came. Rebellion. Clichés. Are you kidding? Drinking.
Do-overs. Cheer-leading Uniforms. Regret. Pure Bliss.
Uncovering. Feeling not good enough. Cockiness. Joy.
In came wild cards. Short skirts. Cocktails. 15. Funnels.
Mid-riff baring. Belly-button rings. Challenges. Being
challenging. The ultimate change. The ultimate fast-forward.
In came growing up.

Bra Shopping

PARNESHIA JONES

Saturday afternoon, Marshall Fields, 2nd floor, women's lingerie please.

At sixteen I am a jeans and t-shirt wearing tomboy who can think of
a few million more places to be instead of in the department store
with my mother bra shopping.

Still growing accustomed to these two new welts
lashed on to me by puberty, getting bigger by the moment,
mother looks at me and says:
While we're here, we'll get some new (larger) shirts for you too.
I resent her for taking me away from baseball fields,
horse play, and riding my bike.

We enter into no man's, and I mean no man in sight land
where women fuss and shop all day for undergarments;
the lingerie department is a world of frilly lace, night gowns,
grandma panties and support everything.

Mama takes me over to a wall covered with hundreds of white bras,
some with lace and little frills or doilies like party favors,
as if undergarments are a cause for celebration.

A few have these dainty ditsy bows in the middle.
That's a nice accent don't you think? Mama would say. *Isn't that cute?*
Like this miniature bow in the middle will take
some of the attention away from what is really going on.

When mama and I go brassiere shopping it never fails:
a short woman with an accent and glasses

attached to a chain around her neck who cares
way too much about undergarments comes up to us.
May I help you, dearies?

The bra woman assists my mother in finding the perfect bra
to as my mother put it, *hold me in the proper way. No bouncing please.*

Working as a team plotting to ruin my entire day
with the bra fitting marathon, they conspire up about ten bras
in each hand which equal forty. Who's making all these bras
   I want to ask.

What size is she? The bra woman asks.
You want something that will support them honey, looking at me with a wink.
My mother looks straight at my chest. *Oh she's good size. She's out of that
training bra phase. I want her to have something that will hold them up proper.*

Them, them, them they say.
Like they're two midgets I keep strapped to my chest.
The whole time I stand there while these two women one my
   own kin,
discuss the maintenance and storage of my two dependents.

The worst is yet to come, the dressing room.
I hate the damn dressing room, the mirrors waiting to laugh at me,
women running in and out half-naked with things showing
that I didn't even see on my own body.

I stand there half-naked and pissed. Mama on one side,
the bra woman on the other, I feel like a rag doll under
   interrogation

as they begin fixing straps, poking me, raising me up, snapping
   the back,
underwire digging my breasts a grave.

The bras clamp down onto me, shaping my breasts out to pristine
   bullets,
with no movement, no pulse, no life, just sitting fix up
like my mother wanted *real proper*.

I will never forgive my mother for this, I keep thinking to myself.
Looking blank face at my reflection I started thinking about how
   my brothers
never have to shop for undergarments, why couldn't I have been
   born a boy?
I hate undergarments.

Mama looks at my face. *Don't you like any of them?*
No, I say. Mama I hate this, please can we go?
Then she goes into her lecture on becoming a woman
and being responsible for woman upkeep.

After we are halfway through the inventory
mama looks at me wasting away in a sea of bras and takes pity
   on me.
All right, I think we have enough to last you for a while. Let's check out.

I don't get happy too quick 'cause I know that bra woman
still lurks about and if she senses my excitement that we are
   leaving
she will come with more white bras.

We make our way to the check out counter
and the bra woman rings us up.
Oh honey you picked out some beautiful bras, she says.
Just remember hand wash. How about bury, I want to ask.

She and my mother talk about how they are just right
and will do the trick for me with no bouncing at all.

Hairwashing

JULIA ALVAREZ

She washed my hair whenever I misbehaved,
ducking my head into a sink of water,
lathering up a head of old man's hair,
short quills, soft fur—
her porcupine, her bear,
her bad bad girl.
"Hold still!" she yelled.

I couldn't. I was growing up
even as she scrubbed for dirt,
horns, anything that looked like sin.
She could not clean inside the bowing head,
tidy the messy loves to come.
She could not set a quarantine on Eden
till she had found the serpent there.
She could not wring desire from my body
or take the curl out of my hair.

The Summer Day

MARY OLIVER

Who made the world?
Who made the swan, and the black bear?
Who made the grasshopper?
This grasshopper, I mean—
the one who has flung herself out of the grass,
the one who is eating sugar out of my hand,
who is moving her jaws back and forth instead of up and down—
who is gazing around with her enormous and complicated eyes.
Now she lifts her pale forearms and thoroughly washes her face.
Now she snaps her wings open, and floats away.
I don't know exactly what a prayer is.
I do know how to pay attention, how to fall down
into the grass, how to kneel down in the grass,
how to be idle and blessed, how to stroll through the fields,
which is what I have been doing all day.
Tell me, what else should I have done?
Doesn't everything die at last, and too soon?
Tell me, what is it you plan to do
with your one wild and precious life?

Living

DENISE LEVERTOV

The fire in leaf and grass
so green it seems
each summer the last summer.

The wind blowing, the leaves
shivering in the sun,
each day the last day.

A red salamander
so cold and so
easy to catch, dreamily

moves his delicate feet
and long tail. I hold
my hand open for him to go.

Each minute the last minute.

I stepped from plank to plank

EMILY DICKINSON

I stepped from plank to plank,
A slow and cautious way;
The stars about my head I felt,
About my feet the sea.

I knew not but the next
Would be my final inch.
This gave me that precarious gait
Some call experience.

to my last period

LUCILLE CLIFTON

well girl, goodbye,
after thirty-eight years.
thirty-eight years and you
never arrived
splendid in your red dress
without trouble for me
somewhere, somehow.

now it is done,
and i feel just like
the grandmothers who,
after the hussy has gone,
sit holding her photograph
and sighing, *wasn't she
beautiful? wasn't she beautiful?*

lumpectomy eve

LUCILLE CLIFTON

all night i dream of lips
that nursed and nursed
and the lonely nipple

lost in loss and the need
to feed that turns at last
on itself   that will kill

its body for its hunger's sake
all night i hear the whispering
the soft

    love calls you to this knife
    for love   for love

all night it is the one breast
comforting the other

Older, Younger, Both

JOYCE SUTPHEN

I feel older, younger, both
at once. Every time I win,
I lose. Every time I count,
I forget and must begin again.

I must begin again, and again I
must begin. Every time I lose,
I win and must begin again.

Everything I plan must wait, and
having to wait has made me old, and
the older I get, the more I wait, and everything
I'm waiting for has already been planned.

I feel sadder, wiser, neither
together. Everything is almost
true, and almost true is everywhere.
I feel sadder, wiser, neither at once.

I end in beginning, in ending I find
that beginning is the first thing to do.
I stop when I start, but my heart keeps on beating,
so I must go on starting in spite of the stopping.

I must stop my stopping and start to start—
I can end at the beginning or begin at the end.
I feel older, younger, both at once.

Survivor

ROGER McGOUGH

Everyday
I think about dying.
About disease, starvation,
violence, terrorism, war,
the end of the world.

It helps
keep my mind off things.

You Can't Have It All

BARBARA RAS

But you can have the fig tree and its fat leaves like clown hands
gloved with green. You can have the touch of a single eleven-
  year-old finger
on your cheek, waking you at one a.m. to say the hamster is back.
You can have the purr of the cat and the soulful look
of the black dog, the look that says, If I could I would bite
every sorrow until it fled, and when it is August,
you can have it August and abundantly so. You can have love,
though often it will be mysterious, like the white foam
that bubbles up at the top of the bean pot over the red kidneys
until you realize foam's twin is blood.
You can have the skin at the center between a man's legs,
so solid, so doll-like. You can have the life of the mind,
glowing occasionally in priestly vestments, never admitting
  pettiness,
never stooping to bribe the sullen guard who'll tell you
all roads narrow at the border.
You can speak a foreign language, sometimes,
and it can mean something. You can visit the marker on the
  grave
where your father wept openly. You can't bring back the dead,
but you can have the words *forgive* and *forget* hold hands
as if they meant to spend a lifetime together. And you can be
  grateful
for makeup, the way it kisses your face, half spice, half amnesia,
  grateful
for Mozart, his many notes racing one another towards joy,
  for towels

sucking up the drops on your clean skin, and for deeper thirsts,
for passion fruit, for saliva. You can have the dream,
the dream of Egypt, the horses of Egypt and you riding in the
    hot sand.
You can have your grandfather sitting on the side of your bed,
at least for a while, you can have clouds and letters, the leaping
of distances, and Indian food with yellow sauce like sunrise.
You can't count on grace to pick you out of a crowd
but here is your friend to teach you how to high jump,
how to throw yourself over the bar, backwards,
until you learn about love, about sweet surrender,
and here are periwinkles, buses that kneel, farms in the mind
as real as Africa. And when adulthood fails you,
you can still summon the memory of the black swan on the pond
of your childhood, the rye bread with peanut butter and bananas
your grandmother gave you while the rest of the family slept.
There is the voice you can still summon at will, like your mother's,
it will always whisper, you can't have it all,
but there is this.

Sign

MARGE PIERCY

The first white hair coils in my hand,
more wire than down.
Out of the bathroom mirror it glittered at me.
I plucked it, feeling thirty creep in my joints,
and found it silver. It does not melt.

My twentieth birthday lean as glass
spring vacation I stayed in the college town
twanging misery's electric banjo offkey.
I wanted to inject love right into the veins
of my thigh and wake up visible:
to vibrate color
like the minerals in stones under black light.
My best friend went home without loaning me money.
Hunger was all of the time the taste of my mouth.

Now I am ripened and sag a little from my spine.
More than most I have been the same ragged self
in all colors of luck dripping and dry,
yet love has nested in me and gradually eaten
those sense organs I used to feel with.
I have eaten my hunger soft and my ghost grows stronger.

Gradually, I am turning to chalk,
to humus, to pages and pages of paper,
to fine silver wire like something a violin
could be strung with, or somebody garroted,
or current run through: silver truly,
this hair, shiny and purposeful as forceps
if I knew how to use it.

The Greatest Love

ANNA SWIR

She is sixty. She lives
the greatest love of her life.

She walks arm-in-arm with her dear one,
her hair streams in the wind.
Her dear one says:
"You have hair like pearls."

Her children say:
"Old fool."

Time

MARY URSULA BETHELL

"Established" is a good word, much used in garden books,
"The plant, when established" . . .
Oh, become established quickly, quickly, garden!
For I am fugitive, I am very fugitive—

Those that come after me will gather these roses,
And watch, as I do now, the white wistaria
Burst, in the sunshine, from its pale green sheath.

Planned. Planted. Established. Then neglected,
Till at last the loiterer by the gate will wonder
At the old, old cottage, the old wooden cottage,
And say, "One might build here, the view is glorious;
This must have been a pretty garden once."

Going Blind

RAINER MARIA RILKE

She sat at tea just like the others. First
I merely had a notion that this guest
Held up her cup not quite like all the rest.
And once she gave a smile. It almost hurt.

When they arose at last, with talk and laughter,
And ambled slowly and as chance dictated
Through many rooms, their voices animated,
I saw her seek the noise and follow after,

Held in like one who in a little bit
Would have to sing where many people listened;
Her lighted eyes, which spoke of gladness, glistened
With outward luster, as a pond is lit.

She followed slowly, and it took much trying,
As though some obstacle still barred her stride;
And yet as if she on the farther side
Might not be walking any more, but flying.

Old Woman

ELIZABETH JENNINGS

So much she caused she cannot now account for
As she stands watching day return, the cool
Walls of the house moving towards the sun.
She puts some flowers in a vase and thinks
   "There is not much I can arrange
In here and now, but flowers are suppliant

As children never were. And love is now
A flicker of memory, my body is
My own entirely. When I lie at night
I gather nothing now into my arms,
   No child or man, and where I live
Is what remains when men and children go."

Yet she owns more than residue of lives
That she has marked and altered. See how she
Warns time from too much touching her possessions
By keeping flowers fed, by polishing
   Her fine old silver. Gratefully
She sees her own glance printed on grandchildren.

Drawing the curtains back and opening windows
Every morning now, she feels her years
Grow less and less. Time puts no burden on
Her now she does not need to measure it.
   It is acceptance she arranges
And her own life she places in the vase.

Let It Be Forgotten

SARA TEASDALE

Let it be forgotten, as a flower is forgotten,
   Forgotten as a fire that once was singing gold,
Let it be forgotten for ever and ever,
   Time is a kind friend, he will make us old.

If anyone asks, say it was forgotten
   Long and long ago,
As a flower, as a fire, as a hushed footfall
   In a long-forgotten snow.

Courage

ANNE SEXTON

It is in the small things we see it.
The child's first step,
as awesome as an earthquake.
The first time you rode a bike,
wallowing up the sidewalk.
The first spanking when your heart
went on a journey all alone.
When they called you crybaby
or poor or fatty or crazy
and made you into an alien,
you drank their acid
and concealed it.

Later,
if you faced the death of bombs and bullets
you did not do it with a banner,
you did it with only a hat to
cover your heart.
You did not fondle the weakness inside you
though it was there.
Your courage was a small coal
that you kept swallowing.
If your buddy saved you
and died himself in so doing,
then his courage was not courage,
it was love; love as simple as shaving soap.

Later,
if you have endured a great despair,

then you did it alone,
getting a transfusion from the fire,
picking the scabs off your heart,
then wringing it out like a sock.
Next, my kinsman, you powdered your sorrow,
you gave it a back rub
and then you covered it with a blanket
and after it had slept a while
it woke to the wings of the roses
and was transformed.

Later,
when you face old age and its natural conclusion
your courage will still be shown in the little ways,
each spring will be a sword you'll sharpen,
those you love will live in a fever of love,
and you'll bargain with the calendar
and at the last moment
when death opens the back door
you'll put on your carpet slippers
and stride out.

DEATH AND GRIEF

*P*OETRY HAS BEEN CALLED "the language of the human heart," and we turn to it when our hearts are breaking. The shock of loss and the pain of grief are physical as well as emotional, and sometimes hard to put into words. Poetry reminds us that these feelings are not unique to us, and by sharing them we can be comforted by our common humanity. Poets face life's most difficult questions head-on and unafraid, and through their work, we find solace and wisdom.

In my family, we have faced a good deal of loss. Each death is different. I know that the times when we have been able to gather at our mothers' bedsides, and hold each other's hands as they pass from life, are a gift we will always treasure. We feel the presence of God. But when we lose someone before their time, it takes the rest of our lives to understand, or to accept that we never will. We can stay connected to their spirit by doing things they enjoyed, caring for those they loved, sharing memories with their friends, and living and working for the things they believed in.

The poems here include matter-of-fact observations about death, like Sappho's fragment "We know this much." Her frank acknowledgment that death is just awful was written twenty-five hundred years ago, yet it speaks directly to us today. The importance of the countless small rituals that accompany death is

captured by Emily Dickinson in her famous poem "The Bustle in a House."

Other poems explore the agony of loss and despair. In "The Widow's Lament in Springtime," William Carlos Williams describes a woman who aches with the desire to surrender life. However, there are more hopeful poems too, like Christina Rossetti's "Remember," which urges us not to be held back by the past, but to move forward with our lives.

As I have moved through the stages of grief in my own life, a healing process occurs. There have been periods during which I have wanted to withdraw from the world. Knowing that my mother turned to poetry at difficult times in her life, and reading the same poems that brought her solace, helped me feel her presence and gave me strength. Later, when I was ready to reengage more fully in the world, poetry helped me remember happy times more often than sad times, feel the guiding spirit of those I have lost, and rely on their memory for a sense of direction and purpose.

We know this much

SAPPHO

Death is an evil;
we have the gods'
word for it; they too
would die if death
were a good thing

The Bustle in a House

EMILY DICKINSON

The Bustle in a House
The Morning after Death
Is solemnest of industries
Enacted upon Earth—

The Sweeping up the Heart
And putting Love away
We shall not want to use again
Until Eternity.

Never More Will the Wind

H. D.

from *Hymen*

Never more will the wind
Cherish you again,
Never more will the rain.

Never more
Shall we find you bright
In the snow and wind.

The snow is melted,
The snow is gone,
And you are flown:

Like a bird out of our hand,
Like a light out of our heart,
You are gone.

Grief

ELIZABETH BARRETT BROWNING

I tell you, hopeless grief is passionless;
That only men incredulous of despair,
Half-taught in anguish, through the mid-night air
Beat upward to God's throne in loud access
Of the absolute Heavens. Deep-hearted man, express
Grief for the Dead in silence like to death—
Most like a monumental statue set
In everlasting watch and moveless woe,
Till itself crumble to the dust beneath.
Touch it; the marble eyelids are not wet.
If it could weep, it could arise and go.

The Widow's Lament in Springtime

WILLIAM CARLOS WILLIAMS

Sorrow is my own yard
where the new grass
flames as it has flamed
often before but not
with the cold fire
that closes round me this year.
Thirtyfive years
I lived with my husband.
The plumtree is white today
with masses of flowers.
Masses of flowers
load the cherry branches
and color some bushes
yellow and some red
but the grief in my heart
is stronger than they
for though they were my joy
formerly, today I notice them
and turn away forgetting.
Today my son told me
that in the meadows,
at the edge of the heavy woods
in the distance, he saw
trees of white flowers.
I feel that I would like
to go there
and fall into those flowers
and sink into the marsh near them.

Companion

JO McDOUGALL

When Grief came to visit,
she hung her skirts and jackets in my closet.
She claimed the only bath.

When I protested,
she assured me it would be
only for a little while.

Then she fell in love with the house,
repapered the rooms,
laid green carpet in the den.

She's a good listener
and plays a mean game of Bridge.
But it's been seven years.

Once, I ordered her outright to leave.
Days later
she came back, weeping.

I'd enjoyed my mornings,
coffee for one;
my solitary sunsets,
my Tolstoy and Molière.

I asked her in.

Remember

CHRISTINA ROSSETTI

Remember me when I am gone away,
    Gone far away into the silent land;
    When you can no more hold me by the hand,
Nor I half turn to go yet turning stay.
Remember me when no more day by day
    You tell me of our future that you planned:
    Only remember me; you understand
It will be late to counsel then or pray.
Yet if you should forget me for a while
    And afterwards remember, do not grieve:
    For if the darkness and corruption leave
  A vestige of the thoughts that once I had,
Better by far you should forget and smile
  Than that you should remember and be sad.

From *To W. P.*

GEORGE SANTAYANA

With you a part of me hath passed away;
For in the peopled forest of my mind
A tree made leafless by this wintry wind
Shall never don again its green array.
Chapel and fireside, country road and bay,
Have something of their friendliness resigned;
Another, if I would, I could not find,
And I am grown much older in a day.
But yet I treasure in my memory
Your gift of charity, and young heart's ease,
And the dear honor of your amity;
For these once mine, my life is rich with these.
And I scarce know which part may greater be—
What I keep of you, or you rob from me.

. . .

To Death

OLIVER ST. JOHN GOGARTY

But for your Terror
Where would be Valour?
What is Love for
   But to stand in your way?
Taker and Giver,
For all your endeavour
You leave us with more
   Than you touch with decay!

That it is a road

ARIWARA NO NARIHARA

That it is a road
Which some day we all travel
I had heard before,
Yet I never expected
To take it so soon myself.

From *In Memoriam A. H. H.*

ALFRED, LORD TENNYSON

XXVII

I envy not in any moods
   The captive void of noble rage,
   The linnet born within the cage,
That never knew the summer woods:

I envy not the beast that takes
   His license in the field of time,
   Unfetter'd by the sense of crime,
To whom a conscience never wakes;

Nor, what may count itself as blest,
   The heart that never plighted troth
   But stagnates in the weeds of sloth,
Nor any want-begotten rest.

I hold it true, whate'er befall;
   I feel it when I sorrow most;
   'Tis better to have loved and lost
Than never to have loved at all.

Reconciliation

WALT WHITMAN

Word over all, beautiful as the sky,
Beautiful that war and all its deeds of carnage must in time be
    utterly lost,
That the hands of the sisters Death and Night incessantly
    softly wash again, and ever again, this soil'd world;
For my enemy is dead, a man divine as myself is dead,
I look where he lies white-faced and still in the coffin—I
    draw near,
Bend down and touch lightly with my lips the white face
    in the coffin.

FRIENDSHIP

*W*HEN I WAS GROWING UP, all I wanted to do was be *with* my friends, be *like* my friends, and dress the same way as my friends did. We all had the same hairstyle and hair color, and mostly we still do. Growing up in a large extended family also gave me a built-in set of people who still know almost everything about me, and taught me how to be a good friend. If we are lucky, we have close friends who have been part of our lives since childhood or college, and others we have connected with through work or through our children. We share relationship dramas, issues at work, health and mothering questions. Now that my children are mostly grown, friends are the ones I turn to for laughter and comfort. One of my favorite lines is in the poem "Girlfriends" by Ellen Doré Watson, who writes of long-term friendships, "The lifers/who, even seven states away, are the porches/*where we land*."

Although female friendships are an important part of our lives, there are not as many poems about female friendship as one might expect. Poets seem to be more concerned with love relationships or their solitary pursuits. However, when they do examine the subject of friendship, they distill its essence. One of the most important qualities in a friendship is that it makes each of us into a better person. "A Poem of Friendship" by Nikki Giovanni and

"Love" by Roy Croft explore this aspect of friendship. Other poems, like "My Friend's Divorce" by Naomi Shihab Nye and "Secret Lives" by Barbara Ras, celebrate the love and support friends give each other during difficult times.

One of my daughters' favorite poems is the dark and startling "A Poison Tree" by William Blake. Blake was ahead of his time in recognizing how important it is to discuss anger and disappointment with our friends, and the dangerous consequences of withholding our feelings.

Once our children have left home (although they say that never really happens), we look for others to care for. I know quite a few middle-aged women who have fallen in love with their pets—and I am one of them. That is why Elizabeth Barrett Browning, known better for her sonnet "How Do I Love Thee? Let Me Count the Ways," is represented here with a poem to her dog, Flush.

And when we run out of friends, there is always "Chocolate" by Rita Dove.

A Poem of Friendship

NIKKI GIOVANNI

We are not lovers
because of the love
we make
but the love
we have

We are not friends
because of the laughs
we spend
but the tears
we save

I don't want to be near you
for the thoughts we share
but the words we never have
to speak

I will never miss you
because of what we do
but what we are
together

Letter to N.Y.

ELIZABETH BISHOP

For Louise Crane

In your next letter I wish you'd say
where you are going and what you are doing;
how are the plays, and after the plays
what other pleasures you're pursuing:

taking cabs in the middle of the night,
driving as if to save your soul
where the road goes round and round the park
and the meter glares like a moral owl,

and the trees look so queer and green
standing alone in big black caves
and suddenly you're in a different place
where everything seems to happen in waves,

and most of the jokes you just can't catch,
like dirty words rubbed off a slate,
and the songs are loud but somehow dim
and it gets so terribly late,

and coming out of the brownstone house
to the gray sidewalk, the watered street,
one side of the buildings rises with the sun
like a glistening field of wheat.

—Wheat, not oats, dear. I'm afraid
if it's wheat it's none of your sowing,
nevertheless I'd like to know
what you are doing and where you are going.

On Gifts for Grace

BERNADETTE MAYER

I saw a great teapot
I wanted to get you this stupendous
100% cotton royal blue and black checked shirt,
There was a red and black striped one too
Then I saw these boots at a place called Chuckles
They laced up to about two inches above your ankles
All leather and in red, black or purple
It was hard to have no money today
I won't even speak about the possible flowers and kinds of
    lingerie
All linen and silk with not-yet-perfumed laces
Brilliant enough for any of the Graces
Full of luxury, grace notes, prosperousness and charm
But I can only praise you with this poem—
Its being is the same as the meaning of your name

Love

ROY CROFT

I love you,
Not only for what you are,
But for what I am
When I am with you.

I love you,
Not only for what
You have made of yourself,
But for what
You are making of me.

I love you
For the part of me
That you bring out;
I love you
For putting your hand
Into my heaped-up heart
And passing over
All the foolish, weak things
That you can't help
Dimly seeing there,
And for drawing out
Into the light
All the beautiful belongings
That no one else had looked
Quite far enough to find.

I love you because you
Are helping me to make

Of the lumber of my life
Not a tavern
But a temple;
Out of the works
Of my every day
Not a reproach
But a song.

I love you
Because you have done
More than any creed
Could have done
To make me good,
And more than any fate
Could have done
To make me happy.

You have done it
Without a touch,
Without a word,
Without a sign.
You have done it
By being yourself.
Perhaps that is what
Being a friend means,
After all.

To Hayley

WILLIAM BLAKE

Thy friendship oft has made my heart to ache:
Do be my enemy—for friendship's sake.

A Poison Tree

WILLIAM BLAKE

I was angry with my friend:
I told my wrath, my wrath did end.
I was angry with my foe:
I told it not, my wrath did grow.

And I water'd it in fears,
Night and morning with my tears;
And I sunned it with smiles,
And with soft deceitful wiles.

And it grew both day and night,
Till it bore an apple bright;
And my foe beheld it shine,
And he knew that it was mine,

And into my garden stole
When the night had veil'd the pole:
In the morning glad I see
My foe outstretch'd beneath the tree.

August

LOUISE GLÜCK

My sister painted her nails fuchsia,
a color named after a fruit.
All the colors were named after foods:
coffee frost, tangerine sherbet.
We sat in the backyard, waiting for our lives to resume
the ascent summer interrupted:
triumphs, victories, for which school
was a kind of practice.

The teachers smiled down at us, pinning on the blue ribbons.
And in our heads, we smiled down at the teachers.

Our lives were stored in our heads.
They hadn't begun; we were both sure
we'd know when they did.
They certainly weren't this.

We sat in the backyard, watching our bodies change:
first bright pink, then tan.
I dribbled baby oil on my legs; my sister
rubbed polish remover on her left hand,
tried another color.

We read, we listened to the portable radio.
Obviously this wasn't life, this sitting around
in colored lawn chairs.

Nothing matched up to the dreams.
My sister kept trying to find a color she liked:

it was summer, they were all frosted.
Fuchsia, orange, mother-of-pearl.
She held her left hand in front of her eyes,
moved it from side to side.

Why was it always like this—
the colors so intense in the glass bottles,
so distinct, and on the hand
almost exactly alike,
a film of weak silver.
ʼ

My sister shook the bottle. The orange
kept sinking to the bottom; maybe
that was the problem.
She shook it over and over, held it up to the light,
studied the words in the magazine.

The world was a detail, a small thing not yet
exactly right. Or like an afterthought, somehow
still crude or approximate.
What was real was the idea:

My sister added a coat, held her thumb
to the side of the bottle.
We kept thinking we would see
the gap narrow, though in fact it persisted.
The more stubbornly it persisted,
the more fiercely we believed.

Summer at the Beach

LOUISE GLÜCK

Before we started camp, we went to the beach.

Long days, before the sun was dangerous.
My sister lay on her stomach, reading mysteries.
I sat in the sand, watching the water.

You could use the sand to cover
parts of your body that you didn't like.
I covered my feet, to make my legs longer;
the sand climbed over my ankles.

I looked down at my body, away from the water.
I was what the magazines told me to be:
coltish. I was a frozen colt.

My sister didn't bother with these adjustments.
When I told her to cover her feet, she tried a few times,
but she got bored; she didn't have enough willpower
to sustain a deception.

I watched the sea; I listened to the other families.
Babies everywhere: what went on in their heads?
I couldn't imagine myself as a baby;
I couldn't picture myself not thinking.

I couldn't imagine myself as an adult either.
They all had terrible bodies: lax, oily, completely
committed to being male and female.

The days were all the same.
When it rained, we stayed home.
When the sun shone, we went to the beach with my mother.
My sister lay on her stomach, reading her mysteries.
I sat with my legs arranged to resemble
what I saw in my head, what I believed was my true self.

Because it *was* true: when I didn't move I was perfect.

Girlfriends

ELLEN DORÉ WATSON

First and last, mirrors
whose secrets we keep in a home-made petrie dish
    (sometimes they give us ideas)
I mean the ones who say the unwelcome when it matters
whose kids watch us for clues
whose kids we watch for clues

Not the ones who decided there was too much too true
    of them in our eyes, and ran,
but the ones who'll be around to see us bald or one-breasted
    and we them
who'll know to say what can't be said (with their skin)
whose bodies, spreading or starved, we love
whose husbands (or lack of) it's okay to disapprove, or almost covet
whose girlfriends are ours by proxy
who share these assumptions and would their last
    Godiva, valium, amulet

The lifers
who, even seven states away, are the porches
where we land

Woman Friend

JULIA ALVAREZ

Before you round the corner and are gone
I wave and note how easily my palm
blots out your car, the motor's hum
merges with Sunday traffic back from church.
You drove up for a weekend visit
to give my life a closer reading,
then catch me up on your story:
both plots, this time, going well,
the heroines about to make big moves
we hope will end with love.

If not, that's what we're friends for.
Late nights or weekends when the rates
go down, we call and splurge on sadness,
bad dreams, or good intentions that become
ambivalent in deed, desires to be saved
in some big way we've learned about in the movies.
Always, we bring up love, either in its past tense
as loss or in its future, longing.
Afraid of weekend loneliness, we meet
and call it since we're women, *friends.*

Before you left, we hugged, promised absolutes
we hope we won't be called to account for
midweek when we're hard at work
earning the living husbands used to pay for
when we were heroines of our mothers' stories.

After you leave, I clean house, fold your bedding,
roll the mattress back into the couch
and tidy any little disorder you created
by being here. Ashamed, I've saved my heart-
breaks for the men who come and go.

My Friend's Divorce

NAOMI SHIHAB NYE

I want her
to dig up
every plant
in her garden,
the pansies, the penta,
roses, rununculas,
thyme and the lilies,
the thing
nobody knows the name of,
unwind the morning glories
from the wire windows
of the fence,
take the blooming
and the almost-blooming
and the dormant,
especially the dormant,
and then
and then
plant them in her new yard
on the other side
of town
and see how
they breathe!

Chocolate

RITA DOVE

Velvet fruit, exquisite square
I hold up to sniff
between finger and thumb—
how you numb me
With your rich attentions!
If I don't eat you quickly,
you'll melt in my palm.
Pleasure seeker, if I let you
you'd liquefy everywhere.
Knotted smoke, dark punch
of earth and night and leaf,
for a taste of you
any woman would gladly
crumble to ruin.
Enough chatter: I am ready
to fall in love!

Magnificat

MICHÈLE ROBERTS

For Sian, after thirteen years

oh this man
what a meal he made of me
how he chewed and gobbled and sucked

in the end he spat me all out

you arrived on the dot, in the nick
of time, with your red curls flying
I was about to slip down the sink like grease
I nearly collapsed, I almost
wiped myself out like a stain
I called for you, and you came, you voyaged
fierce as a small archangel with swords and breasts
you declared the birth of a new life
in my kitchen there was an annunciation
and I was still, awed by your hair's glory

you commanded me to sing of my redemption

oh my friend, how
you were mother for me, and how
I could let myself lean on you
comfortable as an old cloth, familiar as enamel saucepans
I was a child again, pyjamaed
in winceyette, my hair plaited, and you
listened, you soothed me like cakes and milk
you listened to me for three days, and I poured
it out, I flowed all over you

like wine, like oil, you touched the place where it hurt
at night we slept together in my big bed
your shoulder eased me towards dreams

when we met, I tell you
it was a birthday party, a funeral
it was a holy communion
between women, a Visitation

it was two old she-goats butting
and nuzzling each other in the smelly fold

Secret Lives

BARBARA RAS

The same moms that smear peanut butter on bread, sometimes
    tearing
the white center and patching it with a little spit,
the same moms who hold hair back from faces throwing up
    into bowls
and later sit with their kids at bedtime, never long enough at first,
and then inevitably overtime, grabbing on to a hand
as if they could win out against the pull on the other side,
the world's spin and winds and tides,
all of it in cahoots with sex to pull the kid into another orbit,
these moms will go out, maybe in pairs, sometimes in groups,
and leave their kids with dads and fast food, something greasy
they eat with their fingers, later miniature golf, maybe a movie,
a walk with the dog in the dog park,
where one night a kid sees an old mutt riding in a stroller,
invalid, on its back, its paws up, cute like that, half begging,
    half swoon,
and this kid, who once told her mom she knew what dads did
    on poker nights—
"They're guys, they'll just deal the cards and quarrel"—
starts to wonder what moms do out together, whether they talk
    about their kids,
their little rosebuds, their little night-lights,
or are they talking about their bodies and what they did with them
in Portugal, Hawaii, the coast of France, it's better than cards,
it's anatomy and geography, they're all over the map,
or maybe not talking but dancing—
to oldies? light rock? merengue? Would they dare dance

with *men,* with men in vests? in earmuffs? forget earmuffs!
top hats, younger men in sneakers who catch their eye from across
    the room.
Now they're singing. Where have they kept the words to so many
    songs,
storing them up like secrets, hidden candy, the words melting
    in their mouths,
chocolate, caramels, taffy,
the next thing you know they'll be drinking—or are they already
on to a third bottle, some unaffordable Nebbiolo
from the Piedmont, red wine named after the region's fog
and aging into a hint of truffles.
Soon two of them will walk off together, laughing,
their mouths open too wide, their shoulders, no their whole bodies
shaking, the way a bear would laugh after it ate you,
heartily, remorselessly, they laugh all the way to the bathroom,
where together in the mirrors they try to keep a straight face
so they can put on lipstick the crimson of the sun sinking into
    the bay.
They blot their red mouths on tissues they toss
over their shoulders, leaving the impressions of their lips behind
on the floor for a tired woman in a gray dress who'll lift them
    to the trash,
not noticing the moms' lips, not wondering for even a heartbeat
if the kisses there meant hello or good-bye.

To Flush, My Dog

ELIZABETH BARRETT BROWNING

I

Loving friend, the gift of one
Who her own true faith has run
    Through thy lower nature,
Be my benediction said
With my hand upon thy head,
    Gentle fellow creature!

II

Like a lady's ringlets brown,
Flow thy silken ears adown
    Either side demurely
Of thy silver-suited breast,
Shining out from all the rest
    Of thy body purely.

III

Darkly brown thy body is,
Till the sunshine striking this
    Alchemize its dullness,
When the sleek curls manifold
Flash all over into gold,
    With a burnished fullness.

IV

Underneath my stroking hand,
Startled eyes of hazel bland
    Kindling, growing larger,

Up thou leapest with a spring,
Full of prank and curveting,
    Leaping like a charger.

V

Leap! thy broad tail waves a light,
Leap! thy slender feet are bright,
    Canopied in fringes;
Leap—those tasselled ears of thine
Flicker strangely, fair and fine,
    Down their golden inches.

VI

Yet, my pretty, sportive friend,
Little is 't to such an end
    That I praise thy rareness!
Other dogs may be thy peers
Haply in these drooping ears,
    And this glossy fairness,

VII

But of *thee* it shall be said,
This dog watched beside a bed
    Day and night unweary,—
Watched within a curtained room,
Where no sunbeam brake the gloom
    Round the sick and dreary.

VIII

Roses, gathered for a vase,
In that chamber died apace,
    Beam and breeze resigning;

This dog only, waited on,
Knowing that when light is gone
   Love remains for shining.

IX
Other dogs in thymy dew
Tracked the hares and followed through
   Sunny moor or meadow;
This dog only, crept and crept
Next a languid cheek that slept,
   Sharing in the shadow.

X
Other dogs of loyal cheer
Bounded at the whistle clear,
   Up the woodside hieing;
This dog only, watched in reach
Of a faintly uttered speech,
   Or a louder sighing.

XI
And if one or two quick tears
Dropped upon his glossy ears,
   Or a sigh came double,—
Up he sprang in eager haste,
Fawning, fondling, breathing fast
   In a tender trouble.

XII
And this dog was satisfied
If a pale thin hand would glide
   Down his dewlaps sloping,—

Which he pushed his nose within,
After,—platforming his chin
   On the palm left open.

XIII

This dog, if a friendly voice
Call him now to blyther choice
   Than such chamber-keeping,
"Come out!" praying from the door,—
Presseth backward as before,
   Up against me leaping.

XIV

Therefore to this dog will I,
Tenderly not scornfully,
   Render praise and favour:
With my hand upon his head,
Is my benediction said
   Therefore, and for ever.

XV

And because he loves me so,
Better than his kind will do
   Often, man or woman,
Give I back more love again
Than dogs often take of men,
   Leaning from my Human.

XVI

Blessings on thee, dog of mine,
Pretty collars make thee fine,
   Sugared milk make fat thee!

Pleasures wag on in thy tail,
Hands of gentle motion fail
    Nevermore, to pat thee!

XVII
Downy pillow take thy head,
Silken coverlid bestead,
    Sunshine help thy sleeping!
No fly's buzzing wake thee up,
No man break thy purple cup,
    Set for drinking deep in.

XVIII
Whiskered cats arointed flee,
Sturdy stoppers keep from thee
    Cologne distillations;
Nuts lie in thy path for stones,
And thy feast-day macaroons
    Turn to daily rations!

XIX
Mock I thee, in wishing weal?—
Tears are in my eyes to feel
    Thou art made so straitly,
Blessing needs must straiten too,—
Little canst thou joy or do,
    Thou who lovest *greatly*.

XX

Yet be blessèd to the height
Of all good and all delight
   Pervious to thy nature;
Only *loved* beyond that line,
With a love that answers thine,
   Loving fellow creature.

HOW TO LIVE

*I*N COLLEGE, I took a course called Moral and Social Inquiry, taught by the child psychiatrist Dr. Robert Coles. It was considered one of the easiest courses at Harvard because it met at noon and almost everyone got an A. But in fact it was the most challenging, because Dr. Coles asked us to think about the hardest question of all: how to live a life.

Poetry can help us answer that question. It concerns itself with the fundamental questions and reconnects us with our deepest emotions. When everyday life distracts us, poetry can help us feel centered. When the way forward seems blocked and the burdens of work and family overwhelm us, poetry can help us find our voice. This is as true for young women as it is for those of us who are older. People sometimes make the mistake of thinking that poetry is removed or disconnected from life, but Wallace Stevens wrote that the purpose of poetry is "to help people live their lives."

The poems in this section are the reward for having made it through the rest of the book. They encompass all you really need to know. Two of my favorites are "To be of use" by Marge Piercy and "Leap Before You Look" by W. H. Auden. These are the poems that started this book. They were sent to me by a friend at exactly the right time—and reminded me that there is always more to do, and no reason not to do it.

Poetry and prayer are not so different, as we can see from the Shaker hymn "Simple Gifts." Other poems teach us that despite our efforts to control our destiny, our lives are influenced by events larger than ourselves. Poems like "September, 1918" by Amy Lowell and "24th September 1945" by Nazim Hikmet seek to restore hope to a world devastated by war and destruction. Dick Davis's "6 A.M. Thoughts" intertwines humor and acceptance as a strategy for coping with events beyond our control.

Fundamentally, poetry celebrates our individuality and the creative effort of living. The next to last poem in this book was one of my mother's favorites. She loved the ancient Greek attitude toward life—the closeness to nature, the relationship of men and gods, and the reverence for the heroic. Constantine Cavafy, a modern Greek poet who lived a short and tragic life in Alexandria, drew heavily on the ancient myths and history in his work. "Ithaka" is his masterpiece, and it is one of those poems that I carry with me always in my mind.

May 2

DAVID LEHMAN

Someday I'd like to go
to Atlantic City with you
not to gamble (just being
there with you is enough
of a gamble) but to ride
the high white breakers
have a Manhattan and listen
to a baritone saxophone
play a tune called "Salsa
Eyes" with you beside me
on a banquette but why
stop there let's go to
Paris in November when
it's raining and we read
the *Tribune* at La Rotonde
our hotel room has a big
bathtub I knew you'd like
that and we can be a couple
of unknown Americans what
are we waiting for let's go

From a Letter to His Daughter

RALPH WALDO EMERSON

Finish every day and be done with it.
You have done what you could.
Some blunders and absurdities
no doubt have crept in;
forget them as soon as you can.
Tomorrow is a new day;
begin it well and serenely
and with too high a spirit
to be cumbered with
your old nonsense.

This day is all that is
good and fair.
It is too dear,
with its hopes and invitations,
to waste a moment on yesterdays.

To be of use

MARGE PIERCY

The people I love the best
jump into work head first
without dallying in the shallows
and swim off with sure strokes almost out of sight.
They seem to become natives of that element,
the black sleek heads of seals
bouncing like half-submerged balls.

I love people who harness themselves, an ox to a heavy cart,
who pull like water buffalo, with massive patience,
who strain in the mud and the muck to move things forward,
who do what has to be done, again and again.

I want to be with people who submerge
in the task, who go into the fields to harvest
and work in a row and pass the bags along,
who are not parlor generals and field deserters
but move in a common rhythm
when the food must come in or the fire be put out.

The work of the world is common as mud.
Botched, it smears the hands, crumbles to dust.
But the thing worth doing well done
has a shape that satisfies, clean and evident.
Greek amphoras for wine or oil,
Hopi vases that held corn, are put in museums
but you know they were made to be used.
The pitcher cries for water to carry
and a person for work that is real.

Leap Before You Look

W. H. AUDEN

The sense of danger must not disappear:
The way is certainly both short and steep,
However gradual it looks from here;
Look if you like, but you will have to leap.

Tough-minded men get mushy in their sleep
And break the by-laws any fool can keep;
It is not the convention but the fear
That has a tendency to disappear.

The worried efforts of the busy heap,
The dirt, the imprecision, and the beer
Produce a few smart wisecracks every year;
Laugh if you can, but you will have to leap.

The clothes that are considered right to wear
Will not be either sensible or cheap,
So long as we consent to live like sheep
And never mention those who disappear.

Much can be said for social savoir-faire,
But to rejoice when no one else is there
Is even harder than it is to weep;
No one is watching, but you have to leap.

A solitude ten thousand fathoms deep
Sustains the bed on which we lie, my dear:
Although I love you, you will have to leap;
Our dream of safety has to disappear.

Try to Praise the Mutilated World

ADAM ZAGAJEWSKI

Try to praise the mutilated world.
Remember June's long days,
and wild strawberries, drops of wine, the dew.
The nettles that methodically overgrow
the abandoned homesteads of exiles.
You must praise the mutilated world.
You watched the stylish yachts and ships;
One of them had a long trip ahead of it,
while salty oblivion awaited others.
You've seen the refugees heading nowhere,
you've heard the executioners sing joyfully.
You should praise the mutilated world.
Remember the moments when we were together
in a white room and the curtain fluttered.
Return in thought to the concert where music flared.
You gathered acorns in the park in autumn
and leaves eddied over the earth's scars.
Praise the mutilated world
and the grey feather a thrush lost,
and the gentle light that strays and vanishes
and returns.

Leisure

W. H. DAVIES

What is this life if, full of care,
We have no time to stand and stare?

No time to stand beneath the boughs
And stare as long as sheep or cows.

No time to see, when woods we pass,
Where squirrels hide their nuts in grass.

No time to see, in broad daylight,
Streams full of stars, like skies at night.

No time to turn at Beauty's glance,
And watch her feet, how they can dance.

No time to wait till her mouth can
Enrich that smile her eyes began.

A poor life this if, full of care,
We have no time to stand and stare.

The Waking

THEODORE ROETHKE

I wake to sleep, and take my waking slow.
I feel my fate in what I cannot fear.
I learn by going where I have to go.

We think by feeling. What is there to know?
I hear my being dance from ear to ear.
I wake to sleep, and take my waking slow.

Of those so close beside me, which are you?
God bless the Ground! I shall walk softly there,
And learn by going where I have to go.

Light takes the Tree; but who can tell us how?
The lowly worm climbs up a winding stair;
I wake to sleep, and take my waking slow.

Great Nature has another thing to do
To you and me; so take the lively air,
And, lovely, learn by going where to go.

This shaking keeps me steady. I should know.
What falls away is always. And is near.
I wake to sleep, and take my waking slow.
I learn by going where I have to go.

September, 1918

AMY LOWELL

This afternoon was the color of water falling through
    sunlight;
The trees glittered with the tumbling of leaves;
The sidewalks shone like alleys of dropped maple leaves,
And the houses ran along them laughing out of square,
    open windows.
Under a tree in the park,
Two little boys, lying flat on their faces,
Were carefully gathering red berries
To put in a pasteboard box.

Some day there will be no war,
Then I shall take out this afternoon
And turn it in my fingers,
And remark the sweet taste of it upon my palate,
And note the crisp variety of its flights of leaves.
To-day I can only gather it
And put it into my lunch-box,
For I have time for nothing
But the endeavor to balance myself
Upon a broken world.

6 A.M. Thoughts

DICK DAVIS

As soon as you wake they come blundering in
    Like puppies or importunate children;
What was a landscape emerging from mist
    Becomes at once a disordered garden.

And the mess they trail with them! Embarrassments,
    Anger, lust, fear—in fact the whole pig-pen;
And who'll clean it up? No hope for sleep now—
    Just heave yourself out, make the tea, and give in.

A Minor Bird

ROBERT FROST

I have wished a bird would fly away,
And not sing by my house all day;

Have clapped my hands at him from the door
When it seemed as if I could bear no more.

The fault must partly have been in me.
The bird was not to blame for his key.

And of course there must be something wrong
In wanting to silence any song.

May today there be peace within

ST. TERESA OF AVILA

May you trust God that you are exactly where you are meant to be.
May you not forget the infinite possibilities that are born of faith.
May you use those gifts that you have received, and pass on the love that
has been given to you....
May you be content knowing you are a child of God....
Let this presence settle into your bones, and allow your soul the freedom to
sing, dance, praise and love.
It is there for each and every one of us.

The Bacchae Chorus

EURIPIDES

CHORUS

When shall I dance once more
with bare feet the all-night dances,
tossing my head for joy
in the damp air, in the dew,
as a running fawn might frisk
for the green joy of the wide fields,
free from fear of the hunt,
free from the circling beaters
and the nets of woven mesh
and the hunters hallooing on
their yelping packs? And then, hard pressed,
she sprints with the quickness of wind,
bounding over the marsh, leaping
to frisk, leaping for joy,
gay with the green of the leaves,
to dance for joy in the forest,
to dance where the darkness is deepest, where no
    man is.

What is wisdom? What gift of the gods
is held in honor like this:
to hold your hand victorious
over the heads of those you hate?
Honor is precious forever.

Slow but unmistakable
the might of the gods moves on.

It punishes that man,
infatuate of soul
and hardened in his pride,
who disregards the gods.
The gods are crafty:
they lie in ambush
a long step of time
to hunt the unholy.
Beyond the old beliefs,
no thought, no act shall go.
Small, small is the cost
to believe in this:
whatever is god is strong:
whatever long time has sanctioned,
that is a law forever;
the law tradition makes
is the law of nature.

What is wisdom? What gift of the gods
is held in honor like this:
to hold your hand victorious
over the heads of those you hate?
Honor is precious forever.

Blessèd is he who escapes a storm at sea,
    who comes home to his harbor.
Blessèd is he who emerges from under affliction.
In various ways one man outraces another in the race for wealth
    and power.
Ten thousand men possess ten thousand hopes.
A few bear fruit in happiness; the others go awry.
But he who garners day by day the good of life, he is happiest.
Blessèd is he.

The Dawn

W. B. YEATS

I would be ignorant as the dawn
That has looked down
On that old queen measuring a town
With the pin of a brooch,
Or on the withered men that saw
From their pedantic Babylon
The careless planets in their courses,
The stars fade out where the moon comes,
And took their tablets and did sums;
I would be ignorant as the dawn
That merely stood, rocking the glittering coach
Above the cloudy shoulders of the horses;
I would be—for no knowledge is worth a straw—
Ignorant and wanton as the dawn.

Don't Quit

UNKNOWN

When things go wrong, as they sometimes will,
When the road you're trudging seems all up hill,
When the funds are low and the debts are high,
And you want to smile, but you have to sigh,
When care is pressing you down a bit,
Rest, if you must—but don't you quit.

Life is queer with its twists and turns,
As everyone of us sometimes learns,
And many a failure turns about
When he might have won had he stuck it out;
Don't give up, though the pace seems slow—
You might succeed with another blow.

Often the goal is nearer than
It seems to a faint and faltering man,
Often the struggler has given up
When he might have captured the victor's cup.
And he learned too late, when the night slipped down,
How close he was to the golden crown.

Success is failure turned inside out—
The silver tint of the clouds of doubt—
And you never can tell how close you are,
It may be near when it seems afar;
So stick to the fight when you're hardest hit—
It's when things seem worst that you mustn't quit.

All Things Pass

LAO-TZU

All things pass
A sunrise does not last all morning
All things pass
A cloudburst does not last all day
All things pass
Nor a sunset all night
All things pass
What always changes?

Earth ... sky ... thunder ...
   mountain ... water ...
   wind ... fire ... lake ...

These change
And if these do not last

Do man's visions last?
Do man's illusions?

Take things as they come

All things pass

Simple Gifts

ANONYMOUS (SHAKER HYMN)

'Tis the gift to be simple, 'tis the gift to be free,
'Tis the gift to come down where we ought to be,
And when we find ourselves in the place just right,
'Twill be in the valley of love and delight.
When true simplicity is gain'd,
To bow and to bend we shan't be asham'd,
To turn, turn will be our delight
'Till by turning, turning we come round right.

24th September 1945

NAZIM HIKMET

The best sea: has yet to be crossed.
The best child: has yet to be born.
The best days: have yet to be lived;
and the best word that I wanted to say to you
is the word that I have not yet said.

The Journey

MARY OLIVER

One day you finally knew
what you had to do, and began,
though the voices around you
kept shouting
their bad advice—
though the whole house
began to tremble
and you felt the old tug
at your ankles.
"Mend my life!"
each voice cried.
But you didn't stop.
You knew what you had to do,
though the wind pried
with its stiff fingers
at the very foundations—
though their melancholy
was terrible.
It was already late
enough, and a wild night,
and the road full of fallen
branches and stones.
But little by little,
as you left their voices behind,
the stars began to burn
through the sheets of clouds,
and there was a new voice,
which you slowly
recognized as your own,

that kept you company
as you strode deeper and deeper
into the world,
determined to do
the only thing you could do—
determined to save
the only life that you could save.

Ithaka

CONSTANTINE P. CAVAFY

As you set out for Ithaka
hope the voyage is a long one,
full of adventure, full of discovery.
Laistrygonians and Cyclops,
angry Poseidon—don't be afraid of them:
you'll never find things like that on your way
as long as you keep your thoughts raised high,
as long as a rare excitement
stirs your spirit and your body.
Laistrygonians and Cyclops,
wild Poseidon—you won't encounter them
unless you bring them along inside your soul,
unless your soul sets them up in front of you.

Hope the voyage is a long one.
May there be many a summer morning when,
with what pleasure, what joy,
you come into harbors seen for the first time;
may you stop at Phoenician trading stations
to buy fine things,
mother of pearl and coral, amber and ebony,
sensual perfume of every kind—
as many sensual perfumes as you can;
and may you visit many Egyptian cities
to gather stores of knowledge from their scholars.

Keep Ithaka always in your mind.
Arriving there is what you are destined for.
But do not hurry the journey at all.

Better if it lasts for years,
so you are old by the time you reach the island,
wealthy with all you have gained on the way,
not expecting Ithaka to make you rich.

Ithaka gave you the marvelous journey.
Without her you would not have set out.
She has nothing left to give you now.

And if you find her poor, Ithaka won't have fooled you.
Wise as you will have become, so full of experience,
you will have understood by then what these Ithakas mean.

The Colder the Air

ELIZABETH BISHOP

We must admire her perfect aim,
this huntress of the winter air
whose level weapon needs no sight,
if it were not that everywhere
her game is sure, her shot is right.
The least of us could do the same.

The chalky birds or boats stand still,
reducing her conditions of chance;
air's gallery marks identically
the narrow gallery of her glance.
The target-center in her eye
is equally her aim and will.

Time's in her pocket, ticking loud
on one stalled second. She'll consult
not time nor circumstance. She calls
on atmosphere for her result.
(It is this clock that later falls
in wheels and chimes of leaf and cloud.)

ACKNOWLEDGMENTS

I WOULD ESPECIALLY LIKE TO THANK Carrie Bell, Jordan Tamagni, and Bob Hughes for sending me the poems that started this book. All the other poems could not have been found without the help of the amazing Lauren Lipani. I am also grateful to my devoted friend and agent, Esther Newberg, and my editor, Gretchen Young, who makes each project more rewarding than the one before.

This book would not have come into being without the many other people at Hyperion who worked to make it so beautiful—Shubhani Sarkar for the glorious design, David Lott and Claire McKean, who make production miracles happen on a consistent basis, Laura Klynstra for the cover design, Deirdre Smerillo for tracking down runaway poems, and Elizabeth Sabo Morick for help in countless ways. Marie Coolman and Sally McCartin have made a huge difference, and I am grateful for their commitment.

Most of all, I would like to thank my friends and family, who make me happy to get up every morning knowing I might talk to them that day.

CREDITS